new decor

new
decor

Publishing Director Anne Furniss
Creative Director Helen Lewis
Project Editor Zia Mattocks
Picture Researcher Liz Boyd
Assistant Designer Katherine Case
Production Ruth Deary

First published in 2006 by
Quadrille Publishing Limited
Alhambra House
27–31 Charing Cross Road
London WC2H 0LS
www.quadrille.co.uk

Text © 2006 Elizabeth Wilhide
Design and layout © 2006 Quadrille Publishing
Limited

Cataloguing in Publication Data:
a catalogue record for this book
is available from the British Library.

ISBN-13: 978 184400 329 7
ISBN-10: 1 84400 329 9

Printed in China

contents

introduction: the new decor 6

living colour: introducing colour into the home 12
using colour 16
coloured planes 30
broken colour 34
see-through colour 40
coloured light 46
practical colour 52

print room: the new wallpaper 56
wallpaper pattern book 60
print dynamics 68
focal points 72
cover-ups 76
murals 80

material world: textiles, fabrics and other patterned materials 82
material pattern book 86
mix and match 94
comfort zone 98
bedrooms 104
windows 108
floors 112

objects of desire: must-haves, collectables and decorative details 116
lighting 120
21st-century collectables 126
details 132

practicalities: all you need to know 140
planning the work 142
preparing surfaces for decoration 143
painting walls and ceilings 144
papering walls 145
soft furnishings 146
floors 148
lighting 150

stockists and suppliers 153
index 158
acknowledgements 160

introduction

Wallpaper is back; so is the chandelier; and white goods aren't white any longer. A new generation of designers and retailers has restored spirit and vitality to the contemporary interior using vivid colour, bold pattern, decorative details and more than a touch of exuberance. After years when minimal, pared-back, neutrally decorated spaces were presented as the ideal, homes are once again sources of delight and *joie de vivre*. In home decor, pleasure has been neglected for too long.

The new decor isn't about re-creating the past or sidestepping the present. On one hand, traditional forms are given exciting twists using up-to-date imagery and cutting-edge materials and techniques – a baroque chair made of Perspex, a chandelier twinkling with LEDs, a toile de Jouy wallpaper featuring gritty urban scenes. On the other, modernism has not been rejected or left behind, but provides the perfect foil for creative self-expression – a contemporary chair upholstered in a traditional print, for example, or a bold modern light fitting in a room decorated with a retro-print wallpaper.

Ornament is no longer a crime. When you apply decoration to a clean-lined contemporary space, you aren't papering over the cracks, or compensating for any other inadequacies, you're pitting strength with strength. At the same time, you're giving yourself the opportunity to express your own tastes and personality and making room for joy.

Advocates of classic modernism often criticize a more overtly decorative approach to the interior on the grounds that it is fashion-led. But interior styles and fashion have always been closely connected, and never more so than today. Big names in the fashion industry are increasingly turning their hands to the design of patterns that are intended to

be displayed on walls rather than catwalks. The renowned British designer Paul Smith showed that the influence can go the other way when he adopted 'Rajapur', a paisley print designed in the 1950s and recently reissued by Cole & Son, for the detailing of a recent menswear collection. Why shouldn't our homes make us feel as good as our clothes? Why shouldn't our homes make us smile?

Inspiration is one thing, but how do you make it work? One of the key elements of new decor is the mix. In the same way that a great outfit might combine a high-street buy with couture and a vintage accessory, interiors with soul show the same confident blend. Think of a kitchen where the units come from a mass-market retailer, the chairs are vintage and the flooring is solid hardwood. Or a bedroom where an antique French bedstead is the showcase for a riot of vividly patterned bed linen and the walls and floor are plain. Mixing the ingredients in this way creates an interplay of foreground and background that makes interiors come alive.

New decor: less is no longer more.

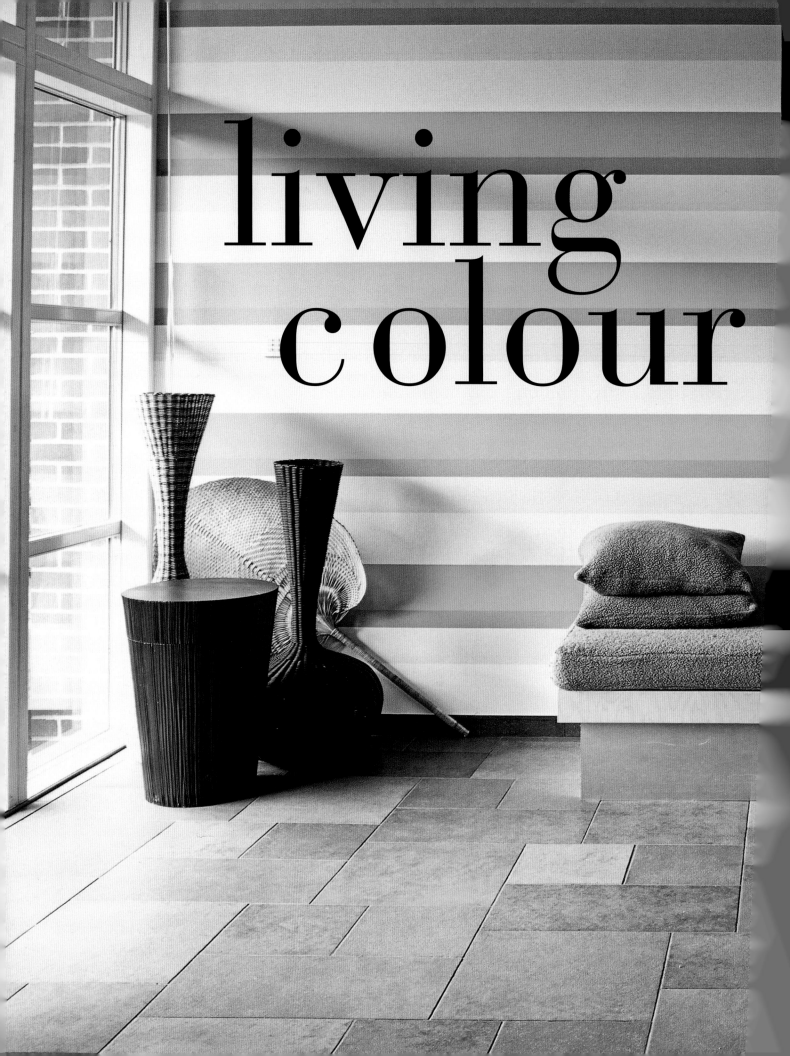

living
colour

Colour is where it all begins. Colour sings, colour is sexy, colour lifts the spirits and feeds the soul. How could we have lived without it for so long?

Until recently, chic modernist interiors were defined by their reticence – pristine white walls, pale wood floors and a tonal palette that ran the whole gamut of, say, biscuit to cream. Homes were as restrained as art galleries without the art, or designer emporia without the stock. Where colour came into the picture at all, it sat uneasily like an intruder, or a party guest who had turned up in the wrong clothes.

No longer. Colour is back, in every shade and hue, and in large enough doses to work its magic. And with the return of this most powerful decorative element has

come a new sophistication. Strong colours are edgy and evocative – think aubergine, cerise, aquamarine, mustard yellow and burnt orange – rather than banal primary shades lifted straight from a paintbox. Soft colours are moody and retro – lilac, pale lemon, blush pink – rather than faint-hearted pastels. Sources of inspiration for contemporary palettes range far and wide, and are as frivolous as fashion.

Colour spells confidence. It's very grown-up. But it's playful, too, speaking to the inner child who hasn't yet thrown up the barriers of taste and would pick a colourful toy over a plain wooden one every time, without hesitation. Time to reach for the paint chart and bring richness and depth, verve and vitality back to the home.

using
colour

Some people just seem to be born with a great eye for colour; most of us have to work at it a little. A good place to start is to think about those shades you find yourself drawn to. They may crop up in your wardrobe or your linen closet; they may sing out from a decorative display. One of the greatest tonics you can give yourself is to live with colours you love.

Accent versus background

Two simple ways of using colour in the rooms of your home are as an accent or as a background. Accent colour says 'look at me'. Background colour says 'feel the mood'.

If you're using colour as an accent, you can either display a single shade in a prominent way, or scatter a number of different colours throughout the interior in the form of details, such as cushions and decorative objects. In both cases, accent colour needs plenty of breathing space.

Background colour is all about creating an atmosphere. That means thinking carefully about the effect you want to create and what you've got to work with. Cool colours, such as blues, blue-greys and violets are soothing and distancing, and make rooms feel more spacious – but they need to be used in settings where there is plenty of natural light, otherwise they will feel chilly. Warm colours, such as reds and oranges, are advancing, enclosing and eye-catching. The energy levels are high, however, so make sure you can stand the heat.

Colour schemes

More complex than using colour as an accent or as a background is to assemble a palette or scheme using a number of colours that work well together. One of the easiest ways of doing this is to exploit the inherent resonance of complementary pairs, or those colours that sit opposite each other on the colour wheel: for example, blue and orange, red and green, and yellow and purple.

Complementary colours mixed together in varying degrees produce very subtle shades; add white or black and the result is a series of harmonious graduated tones. You can use the lightest shade for backgrounds, such as walls, and the darkest or most intense for details and accents. Play around with scale and proportion – you can always place two strong colours next to each other if one covers a large expanse and the other is restricted to trim, edging or detail.

You can also gain inspiration for a colour scheme from a patterned fabric, rug, favourite picture or even an item of clothing – ready-made palettes, if you like. Alternatively, keep a cuttings file of samples, swatches and tear sheets from interiors magazines that feature colours or colour combinations that appeal to you and draw on this source for decorating ideas.

nature palette

✿ Green is going places. Maybe it's the continuing love affair with all things retro, or maybe it's a case of wearing our eco-awareness on our walls, but tonal shades of green are decidedly of the moment. Forget eye-watering acid lime or soporific forest green: these soft, subtle leafy shades suggest the heartening sight of new spring growth crossed with a dash of oriental elegance and refinement for good measure.

✿ Green is as good as a rest. Because the colour corresponds to the light waves in the middle of the visible spectrum, our eyes do not have to adjust very much to see it, which is why green is so calming and restful.

✿ Accent grey-green walls with straw yellow. Anchor green schemes with dark brown for a graphic look. Natural surfaces and finishes such as rattan, stained floorboards and organic weaves work well with green, too, as do contemporary leafy printed textiles.

✿ The nature palette suits sunny, airy rooms. But beware of using strong shades of green on the walls, as the effect can be rather bilious and unflattering.

bright palette

✳ Bring instant happiness into your home with bright, singing colour. These shades – blue-green, orangey red, sky blue and sunshine yellow – have all the energy of a Latin American carnival, full of gaiety and *joie de vivre*. Because they aren't primaries, but hover on the cusp of one colour and the next, they have a luminous quality that shifts with changes of the light, which also gives them a natural affinity with one another.

✳ Use blocks of bright colour next to each other for a resonating effect.

✳ Overbright is overkill. Make sure you allow some breathing space – a neutral floor to unify the whole scheme, or neutral walls to offset furniture, cushions and rugs decked to the nines in strong colour.

dark palette

Deep, bruised colours such as aubergine, slate and mahogany make a rich, brooding backdrop with a strong retro feel. Take inspiration from chic, sophisticated nightspots and cocktail bars and soak up the mood.

Black is the new black. Add baroque touches with dark brocades or glossy lacquered pieces. Matt black walls can be sumptuous, but they must be properly prepared and perfectly smooth.

Dark materials such as slate, granite and dark stained floorboards bring depth of character to the mix.

Offset rooms decorated in dark colours with plainer, lighter areas, otherwise you'll feel as if you're living under a stone.

metal palette

✳ Metallic surfaces are glitzy and atmospheric. Part colour, part texture, the heart of their appeal is the reflective shimmer that gives depth of character to surfaces and finishes. The inevitable association is with the luxury of precious metals such as gold and silver.

✳ Metallic schemes don't have to cost the earth. On walls and furniture alike, specialist metallic paints or foil papers will do the trick. Commercial gold- and silver-leaf kits are also available. These do not contain precious metals, so they are a surprisingly affordable option for creating this look. Gloss paint on the floor adds glamour.

✳ Accent metallic schemes with strong statement colours such as Chinese red or clear yellow. Matt black provides a striking graphic contrast. Accessorize with burnished metallic objects or light shades and plenty of mirror.

Gold and silver leaf

Gold- and silver-leaf finishes on walls or ceilings can be achieved using kits available from art and craft stores. These provide the materials you need, including books of sheets about 10cm square, and contain no precious metals.

1 For best results, line walls with wallpaper first, then apply a base coat. Red is the traditional base coat colour for gold leaf, but dark brown or black can also be very effective.

2 Once the paint is dry, apply a coat of size to the wall.

3 Gently roll out a sheet of gold or silver leaf over the surface. Brush it in place with a paintbrush.

4 Once the entire wall is covered with the sheets of gold or silver leaf, rub the surface gently with a cloth. Where flakes of the gold or silver leaf drop off, the base colour will be revealed.

Metallic paint

❀ For an alternative metal finish, paint metalwork and radiators with metallic paints, such as Hammerite, that dry to a textured finish.

❀ Special rollers are available for applying metallic wall paints. These produce a texture like beaten metal.

❀ Metallic spray paint for cars can be used on reclaimed metal filing cabinets and similar items. Work outdoors and wear a face mask to avoid inhaling the fumes.

coloured planes

One of the easiest ways to give an instant lift to your surroundings is to pick out a wall or a portion of a wall in a single shade. Such vivid planes or 'feature walls' represent a halfway point between using colour as accent and colour as background. You get the best of both worlds – the effect is not as dominant as painting all the walls, but has more impact than coloured displays.

Treating a wall as a plane of colour works well in contemporary interiors where traditional architectural detailing is minimal or absent. In open-plan or multipurpose areas, planes of colour can be used to define zones of activity – forming a backdrop to an eating area or a kitchen, for example. Colour will always draw the eye, so it's best if you give it a reason to be there.

Alternatives to single walls include chimney breasts, alcoves and recesses. A similar effect can be achieved by restricting strong colour to a hallway to create a bright thread that connects different parts of the home. Whatever the location, the best results will be achieved on pristine plasterwork.

Choosing paint

Commercial paint ranges appear to offer a huge breadth of choice – every conceivable colour under the sun. If you examine a paint chart or collection of swatches more closely, however, you may notice that these seemingly endless variations are often tonal – lighter or darker shades of the same basic colour.

Before you go shopping for paint, equip yourself with a collection of cuttings or samples of the colours that appeal to you. If you can't find an exact match, don't worry. Some specialist suppliers will mix paint to your own specification; one manufacturer guarantees to produce paint to match any one of the internationally recognized Pantone colours.

Printed squares on paint charts and colourbooks tell only part of the story. With paint, as with any other decorative ingredient, you get what you pay for. Pigment is what gives depth and richness of colour; it is also the most expensive component of paint. Therefore, the more expensive the paint, the more likely you are to achieve a finish that is truly saturated and glowing. By contrast, cheap mass-market emulsions, which contain less pigment, tend to produce flat, lifeless colours.

Using sample pots

Always test colours *in situ*. Many colours 'mount up', which means they appear much stronger on the wall than they do in the pot. Once you have made your choice, buy a sample pot and paint an area of the wall to assess how the colour looks. It's a good idea to live with the colour for a while to see how it appears under different light conditions. If you haven't yet decided which wall you want to decorate, paint a couple of drops of lining paper and pin these up in different locations.

Surfaces and finishes

Paint finishes range from matt emulsion through silky eggshell to shiny, reflective gloss. Specialist floor paints are also available that are more hard-wearing than paints produced for walls and trim. Concrete can be painted without sealing; wooden floors are best sealed first with a couple of layers of aluminium-based undercoat.

Vinyl, lino, tile, rubber and carpeting are other ways of introducing colour as a continuous floor-level plane to unify different areas. The same strategy of living with a sample before you commit yourself to a purchase applies. Flooring is more expensive than paint and more disruptive to change: you don't want to find the colour is wrong once the floor is laid.

broken colour

The new broken colour represents a complete departure from the type of paint effect, common 20 years ago, which resulted in clouded, mottled, textural finishes. Unlike ragging, sponging or stippling, today's crisp, sharp-edged effects are essentially geometric and are designed to complement the clean lines of contemporary interiors, rather than form the muted backdrop to period-style decor. Like coloured planes, broken colour, in the form of bold spots, stripes, oblongs or similar shapes, demands a perfectly smooth background – these are not wall treatments that are tolerant of imperfection.

The effect need not be limited to walls alone. Geometric motifs can add a vivid graphic punch to a whole range of different elements in the interior, from kitchen counters to blinds and screens.

Stripes

☀Stripes are strongly directional. They naturally lead the eye up or along and therefore serve to adjust proportions visually in the same way as striped articles of clothing can accentuate or disguise different body shapes. Using stripes vertically in the interior makes a room seem higher. Using stripes horizontally lowers the ceiling and has a more calming effect.

☀Stripes don't have to be straight, though they should always have neat, crisp edges. Curved bands have a retro appeal in keeping with 1960s- and 1970s-style interiors.

☀Stripes don't have to be the same width. Varying bands of colour suggest the effect of jaunty deck-chair material and similar designs.

☀Gain inspiration for colourways from natural weaves, such as ticking or Madras cotton, or choose colours to tone with furnishings and wall and flooring colours.

☀New stripy designs in laminate or melamine make groovy kitchen counters and splashbacks.

How to create a striped pattern

As a geometric design, stripes must be neatly executed – no wobbly or hesitant lines or uneven patches of colour. You will need to equip yourself with a long straight edge, a measuring tape, and masking tape or card.

1 Measure the area of wall that you intend to decorate. Draw up a scale plan of the wall on graph paper.

2 Work out your design on paper first. If you want even bands, divide up the wall area accordingly. If you want stripes of varying widths, play around with the design to see what looks best. Use coloured pencils, pens or paints to gauge the effect.

3 To transfer the design to the wall, measure the depth of each stripe at regular intervals across the wall and, using a long straight edge, draw pencil guidelines on the wall.

4 To ensure stripes are straight and even, mask the edges with masking tape or a piece of card before you paint.

How to create a spotty pattern

As is the case with stripes, spots must be neatly executed – you want crisp circles not blobs. The best way of achieving this is to create a circle template from a stiff sheet of card and use it as a stencil.

1 Measure the area of wall that you intend to decorate. Draw up a scale plan of the wall on graph paper.

2 Work out your design on paper first, playing around with spacing. Spots do not necessarily have to be perfectly equidistant, but it is a good idea to space them as evenly as possible.

3 Experiment with colour patterns using coloured pencils, pens or paints to gauge the effect.

4 Mark out the position of each spot on the wall using a pencil.

5 Position the circle template so that the pencil mark is at the centre of the template and paint the spot on the wall.

Spots

There's something irresistible about spotty patterns. As a geometric motif, spots are perfectly in tune with the sleek lines of contemporary interiors. At the same time, the sheer light-hearted nature of the design serves to undercut high-minded architectural seriousness. Create a feature wall of spots for your own Damien Hirst-style artwork.

Pay attention to scale. If you want to repeat a number of spots across a wall, they should be large enough to have an impact – say 10cm or so in diameter; if they're much smaller your wall will look as if it has broken out in a rash. Very large spots or circles are also highly effective but can be a little trickier to execute.

see-through colour

Translucent or transparent coloured materials are an evocative way of combining colour with light. Colour gains added intensity when light is shone through it – think of the jewel-like richness of stained-glass windows.

Coloured glass

Panels of coloured glass tint the light in intriguing ways. Fanlights over doors, both internal and external, are ripe for this treatment. The same is true for glazed extensions – coloured glass panes at a high level cast beautiful patches of tinted light on walls and floor that shift according to the position of the sun in the sky. All you have to do is contact a glazier who stocks coloured glass and supply measurements for the openings in question. Coloured glass also serves a practical function in areas where privacy is required but you don't want to block light altogether, such as bathrooms.

For a more decorative effect, consult a stained-glass artist and commission an original design. And remember that stained glass doesn't have to be historical in style – geometric or abstract contemporary designs are highly effective.

Coloured partitions

In open-plan or multipurpose areas it can be difficult to separate different activities without compromising the overall sense of space. Solid sliding partitions are one answer, but they do block light, which can be a disadvantage, particularly if space is restricted and there are limited openings. Fully transparent partitions, on the other hand, don't provide much visual separation and can be hazardous – a large sheet of glass can be nigh-on invisible. One solution is to make a partition from a large panel of coloured glass or Perspex, a strategy that will provide the requisite separation while letting the light through. At the same time, a coloured translucent partition works very much like a coloured wall plane and forms a vivid decorative focus in its own right.

You can also adapt the same idea to screen fitted storage. In a pared-down interior, clear glass is too revealing of cupboard clutter. Coloured glass, acrylic or Perspex removes the detail from the picture and abstracts cupboard contents to shapes and silhouettes.

❀ Many period properties incorporate panels of coloured glass. Typical locations for such decorative features include external doors and landing windows. If you have such original details, you can base a contemporary decorative scheme around the colours to create a successful marriage of old and new.

Details

✳ See-through colour is just as effective in small doses as it is on a grander scale. Coloured glass or fabric shades turn ordinary lamps and light fittings into glowing focal points.

✳ Small acrylic or Perspex coloured panels can be fitted into the top or base of built-in storage units and backlit to help dematerialize the bulk of such features. At a low level, backlit panels make fitted storage appear to float over the floor.

✳ Window treatments provide scope for exploiting the evocative effect of light and colour. Strips of coloured acrylic hung like a bead curtain in front of a window tint the light and cast intriguing patterns on the walls and floor. Sheets of coloured gel can be applied directly to window panes for a mosaic effect.

Light is a feel-good factor in its own right; with colour it offers the potential to create evocative shifts of mood and atmosphere. Recent technological developments mean that now the light source itself can be coloured, which widens the decorative possibilities considerably. Coloured sources suitable for use in the home include LEDs (light-emitting diodes) and coloured fluorescent tubes. Neon, the coloured light source of commercial signage, requires high voltages to operate and specialist installation, making it less acceptable for domestic use. Cold cathode, a low-voltage, very long-lasting light source, has a hefty price tag and must also be professionally installed.

Coloured fluorescent tubes

Until recently, fluorescents were only available in white and the light they emitted had an unpleasant, greenish cast. Nowadays fluorescent tubes come in a range of soft colours including rose, blue and green. Relatively cheap, readily available and requiring no specialist installation, coloured fluorescent tubes are a user-friendly way of exploring the potential of coloured light.

Concealed behind baffles or in recesses, coloured fluorescent tubes produce a defining line of coloured light that can be used to accentuate architectural detail. Mounting them behind glass or Perspex creates a more diffuse glow. Because they generate very little heat, they can be safely used in close proximity to flammable materials. Fluorescent tubes have a lifespan of 8,000 hours and are very energy efficient. Coloured gels can be used to tint the light from plain fluorescent tubes.

LEDs

Winking away in display panels, indicators and other forms of instrumentation, LEDs have long proved their practical usefulness in scores of products. These tiny light sources emit hardly any heat, consume minimal energy and last for up to 100,000 hours. Many lighting experts believe that LEDs may effectively replace low-voltage sources altogether in the not-too-distant future.

Recently, LEDs have found a new decorative role in home lighting systems as a result of improvements that have increased their brightness and extended the colour range. Previously available in red, orange, amber, yellow and green, LEDs now come in blue and white, considerably widening the creative possibilities. These formerly pricey lights are also becoming more affordable, with many products available in mass-market outlets.

coloured
light

Colourwashing

Interactive colour-changing systems using LEDs can be set to wash walls with a single colour or in a rainbow sequence of light, either randomly or in a prearranged programme. This type of colourwashing is most effective when directed at smooth white planes. Many of these systems are increasingly affordable: for less than half the price of a new sofa you can bathe a living area or bedroom in changing colour – instant redecoration at the touch of a button. Colourwashing is also a great way of picking out an alcove or recess.

Bathe in colour

In addition to the ambient effects created by colourwashing systems, there are also bathtubs, sinks and shower cubicles on the market that incorporate LED ports so that water is illuminated with coloured light. Like those systems designed for room use, these can be set to a single colour or to a sequence.

Paths of colour

Floor tiles are available inset with either white or coloured LEDs to create rainbow effects underfoot. Wall tiles incorporating LEDs are also new on the market. Because this light source is so long-lasting, you won't need to replace the tiles for years.

Ambient colour

The most successful lighting schemes rely principally on concealed sources, so that what you see is light diffused over surfaces, not individual lights. The same is true when you are using coloured light sources. Conceal the source of the light and direct it so that surrounding surfaces are bathed in an ambient glow. In minimal spaces, where surfaces are natural or display a fairly restricted tonal palette, coloured light can provide just enough theatricality to lift surroundings out of the ordinary. The bonus, as with all lighting effects, is that you don't have to live with them every day if you don't want to. Coloured light is inherently low level – it's not sufficiently bright to serve as background light on its own. Make sure you put all lights on dimmer controls, so you can vary the effect according to need and mood.

practical colour

When labour-saving domestic appliances first became widely available and affordable in the 1950s, they were universally produced in white. For the ordinary consumer, who had to be persuaded that it was worth investing in such products, white spelled out a message of reliability, efficiency and hygiene.

Today, you have only to stray into a kitchen department to appreciate that the term 'white goods' has all but lost its relevance. Refrigerators, dishwashers and cooking ranges are uniformly white no longer, but come in a variety of shades from pillar-box red to midnight blue. Nowadays, we trust enough in technology to welcome a wider colour choice. Besides which, there's something curiously appealing and irreverent about a baby-blue fridge.

A similar decorative shift has occurred when it comes to other fixtures and fittings in the home. While the avocado bathroom suite remains an all-time low point in decorative taste, colour is creeping back into the bathroom again. Tubs and sinks may remain pristine white, but coloured cladding introduces a vitalizing accent that brings bathrooms to life.

Kitchen colour

As the kitchen has increasingly become the focus of contemporary living, accommodating a wide variety of roles beyond the essential function of food preparation and storage, the range of decorative choices has expanded enormously, and colour has burst on the scene in a previously unimaginable way. Colour is hugely uplifting and there's no reason why we should forgo this powerful decorative element in a room where we spend a great deal of time. However, it's important to put a scheme together carefully. Too much of a visual assault and the kitchen will cease to function as a comfortable place to prepare and enjoy food.

Remember that fridges and ranges are big purchases and you will have to live with them for some time. Similarly, fitted units are not replaced every day. Opt for what makes your heart sing the most – a run of glossy red cupboards or a blush-pink fridge – and keep the rest relatively restrained.

Doors, drawers and decor panels

One of the cheapest and simplest ways of injecting new life into tired fitted kitchens is to change the doors, decor panels and drawer fronts. As most carcasses of fitted units come in standard sizes, it's easy to source new doors, panels and drawer fronts from kitchen suppliers. Alternatively, you could commission a carpenter to make up some new doors for you in an inexpensive material such as MDF (medium-density fibreboard). This composite man-made wood is dimensionally very stable and will not warp. It's also easy to paint.

Even melamine or laminate doors can be painted if you don't want to go to the trouble of having new doors made. Remove the doors completely and rough up the surface with sandpaper to provide a key for the paint, then wipe down with a soft cloth. Paint the doors inside and out with undercoat, and then apply a wipable topcoat in a water-resistant oil-based paint.

Parapan® is an exciting new material made of solid acrylic that can be used for cupboard fronts or any vertical surface. The material is waterproof, hygienic and through-coloured; it comes in 20 shades and can be polished to a high gloss.

print
room

58

For many years, style-conscious home decorators would have cheerfully echoed Oscar Wilde's last words: 'Either that wallpaper goes, or I do.' In the great modernist purge of the late twentieth century, interiors were stripped bare of every last vestige of printed paper and pattern, with much ruthless determination and application of elbow grease. All this has changed with a vengeance. The dramatic return of wallpaper is one of the most exciting developments on the decorative scene today.

Wallpaper has attitude. New trends in design are being pushed from both the art world and the fashion industry, while the range of papers with a contemporary twist is expanding every season. From quirky designs produced in small runs by modern artists exploring interactivity, new materials and digital technology, to the reinvention of motifs plundered from the archives, the print room has never shown such flair or sophistication.

Paper is indisputably the classic medium for delivering pattern to walls. Historically, however, wallpaper itself began as an affordable imitation of fine fabrics such as damask and brocade, which were often used to cover walls in grand or palatial settings. Nowadays, the exchange is a busy two-way street, with most wallpaper patterns subsequently issued in fabric and many traditional fabric designs reappearing as wallpaper.

Evidence of the creative crossover comes from fashion labels such as Paul Smith, Stella McCartney and Juicy Couture, all of which have used papers from distinguished wallpaper producers Cole & Son to decorate their shops, showrooms and headquarters. And with fashion designers such as Matthew Williamson, Eley Kishimoto and Barbara Hulanicki (ex-Biba) turning their hand to wallpaper design, the message is clear. Wallpaper is nothing less than couture for the home.

WALLPAPER PATTERN BOOK

revival

Many of the new wallpapers on the market hark back to traditional designs – in more ways than one. Long-established wallpaper producers have ransacked their archives and updated period designs with contemporary colourways, or have blown up the scale of the motif for a more dramatic, edgy look – classics with a twist, if you like. Delving less far back into the past are manufacturers of reissued designs by twentieth-century greats such as Florence Broadhurst. In addition, there are new papers by leading fashion names such as Matthew Williamson and Barbara Hulanicki, proof positive of creative cross-fertilization.

modern floral

Floral wallpaper used to be synonymous with the country-cottage look – small-scale sprigged prints on the bedroom walls to go with the roses growing over the door. Modern florals have none of that shy reticence, and if they're feminine, it's an urban, sophisticated glamour that they project, rather than a dainty, faded prettiness. Overscaled motifs are the key, as well as strong colours that are sometimes decidedly nonfloral. While many of these designs do retain an air of the boudoir about them, others are handsome enough to work well in living areas, too.

WALLPAPER PATTERN BOOK

monochrome

Nothing packs a greater punch than monochromatic prints. Many wallpaper designs consist of a single colour printed over a white ground; these examples have additional impact through the strength of the contrast, which really draws the eye. A monochromatic print has a certain architectural quality that makes it relatively easy to introduce into a contemporary interior that is otherwise lacking in pattern. Designs vary from the abstract and graphic to more illustrative and pictorial motifs. Don't expect such designs to fade into the background, however: they need to be the focus of attention.

WALLPAPER PATTERN BOOK

graphic

Just because a pattern is graphic does not mean it sits outside time. Many contemporary graphic designs have a distinctly retro feel, harking back to the psychedelic swirls of the 1960s, or to more rectilinear 1970s motifs in appropriate colourways. Textured and metallic finishes add a degree of depth to a graphic pattern – modern foils are considerably improved and are less prone to creasing than earlier examples. When choosing a graphic print, decide whether you want a design that is inherently orderly or one that displays a greater degree of movement.

print dynamics

Repetition is what gives printed patterns their dynamic quality. We're naturally attracted to pattern – it's there in the living world and it's at the heart of creative endeavour. Like music, visual pattern is all about order and harmony. It can be intricate and detailed, or jazzy and free-flowing, but the beat of repetition is what holds it together.

One of the greatest pattern designers of all time, William Morris held strict views about the application of pattern in the interior. He believed that symmetrical designs were best suited for papers, as these would be displayed flat on the wall, while more naturalistic or 'branching' designs were best for fabric, which is gathered or hung in folds. Morris's designs remain some of the best-loved patterns in the history of decoration – but from the vantage point of the twenty-first century we can afford to relax the rules a little about how and where they are used.

Scale and proportion

One of the most significant features of contemporary wallpaper design is the increased size and scale of the repeat. Wallpaper is no longer lurking in the background: it's big, blowsy and overblown. The reinvention of wallpaper has partly been driven by artists such as Tracy Kendall, whose early designs featured large-scale images of single feathers and cutlery. Contemporary collections from traditional producers have included archive patterns blown up in scale, so that the motif assumes greater importance as a pictorial element. The relationship between motif and background is subtly altered, so that the print appears open and airy rather than dense and textural.

Big bold motifs suit small enclosed spaces very well. Large patterns are less overwhelming in areas such as bathrooms and halls because wall space is more limited; these rooms tend to be experienced for shorter periods, too. There is also something irreverent about featuring a large design in a small space – you are defying the limited scale rather than making excuses for it.

Colour and texture

New patterns feature edgy, up-to-the-minute colourways that resonate on the eye. Pinks, limes and purples give genteel period designs instant modern glamour. High-end papers can also be commissioned in custom colours to tone with an existing decorative scheme.

Textured papers such as flocks and foils have renewed sex appeal in today's chic interiors. The technique of flocking paper dates back to the late seventeenth century; recent technological developments give contemporary flocks a soft, velvety texture. In bold graphic colours, the effect is both tailored and baroque. Reflective foils are equally eye-catching. Depending on the pattern, they may evoke the futuristic decor of the mid-twentieth century, 1960s psychedelia or 1970s glam rock. The shimmering quality of these papers is very light-enhancing, and the use of optical inks creates stunning luminous effects that change with the light.

focal points

Using wallpaper to create a focal point is akin to picking out a wall as a plane of colour. For those who are new to the use of pattern, and perhaps a little nervous of it, this strategy is a good entry point. It's also affordable – high-quality wallpapers can be very expensive. Displaying wallpaper as a focal point allows you to enjoy the vitality of pattern without blowing your budget.

Papering a single wall, or a portion of a wall, displays the pattern like a painting and gives a room a strong visual identity. As with coloured planes, the focal point needs a reason to be there. You can use paper to create a feature wall or to anchor the furniture arrangement – as the backdrop to an eating area, for example, or as a graphic bedhead. Alternatively, you can accentuate architectural detail by papering an alcove – the effect is similar to lining a sober suit in an exuberant patterned material. Papered or patterned room dividers inject character and personality into open-plan layouts.

The key is to use strong designs that are relatively large in scale. A pattern that has a small repeat won't do the trick – it will simply look as if you haven't got around to papering the rest of the room.

Types of wall coverings

Paper This is the standard cover-up for walls. Quality varies widely and, as with other decorative elements, you get what you pay for. At the top end of the market are hand-printed papers produced using wood blocks – in general, the more colours that are featured in the pattern, the greater the expense. Features such as hand-gilding or the use of optical inks may also increase cost. Screen-printed papers are good quality, too. The least expensive are machine-printed designs. Many wallpaper companies also produce designs in foil or flock.

Art-house Wallpapers from artist-designers are generally produced in short runs. Some recent examples include 'interactive' designs such as Linda Florence's 'Morphic Damask', which features a pattern that changes when you rub up against it, and Rachel Kelly's 'Long Flower' wallpaper panels, where the basic hand-printed design can be customized with lace-cut vinyl stickers of flowers and foliage (the same stickers are available in transparent plastic for application to glass).

Natural fibres Textured papers have come a long way since the days of Lincrusta and Anaglypta (the Artexes of the paper world). Natural fibres such as grass, sisal, jute, rattan and hessian are available backed with paper and can be applied to the wall in the same way as regular wallpaper. While these lack the exuberance of contemporary designs, they do provide a subtle depth of character.

Cork Another variation on the theme are cork-backed tiles featuring photographic designs digitally printed on paper and coated with vinyl to provide a durable waterproof finish. While these were originally produced as floor tiles, they can also be applied to the wall.

Fabric Coming full circle, fabric is once again finding favour as a luxurious wall treatment. Fabric gives unique depth to walls. Grand and refined, yet warm and intimate, too, it introduces an element of softness to the interior, while at the same time providing additional sound insulation. Traditional fabrics for upholstering walls include silk damask, which is naturally very expensive. Alternatives are furnishing cottons and linen.

Like wallpaper, you can use fabric either to cover a panel, room divider or partition, or to stretch across the wall as a decorative backdrop. One of the most straightforward means of application is simply to stretch and staple the fabric in place, concealing the staples with a braiding, ribbon or other trim. There are also invisible fixings on the market now that obviate the need for trim. The traditional method, however, which results in a softer and more tailored result, is to attach the fabric to plywood battens, with the gap between the fabric and the wall filled with 'bump', a soft wadding or curtain interlining. The technique demands expertise: you need to make sure that each drop of fabric matches the one next to it exactly – and error is costly.

✴ Patterns that have a white background can be displayed as a focal point on white walls. In the case of patterns where the ground is coloured, pick out the background colour of the paper and paint the rest of the room the same shade for a blended, harmonious look.

✴ Choose water-resistant papers for areas that are likely to get wet or be exposed to steamy conditions, such as bathrooms and kitchens.

✴ If you are emphasizing a room divider with pattern, you could cover each side of the partition in the same pattern, but in a different colourway.

✴ Double-width papers provide seamless coverage for alcoves or feature walls.

A contributing factor in wallpaper's fall from grace was the fact that it was often used in a remedial fashion, to paper over battered walls and poor plasterwork. Cosmetic cover-ups don't really fool the eye. A beautiful pattern deserves smooth, properly prepared walls and crisp detailing.

cover-ups

A patterned room is a world of its own. Covering all the walls in the same design creates a sense of enclosure and intimacy. This kind of enveloping effect is ideally suited to rooms that are self-contained. In an open-plan layout, where different areas remain visible, make sure you leave walls plain in part of the space to avoid too great a degree of visual assault.

When using pattern to this extent, it's often best to opt for either smaller repeats or less insistent colourways, so that the result is not too overwhelming. But bold designs can also be very effective, provided that you keep the rest of the furnishings fairly restrained.

Coordination

Along with the return of pattern has come a renewed interest in creating coordinated interiors, where the same design is repeatedly used over several different surfaces. Coordinated schemes can be charming and soothing but you need to avoid overkill, otherwise the effect will simply be smothering or twee. One approach is to match the design of curtains and wallpaper and keep everything else in the room relatively plain. Another is to partner a busy wallpaper with a fabric that features the same colours and similar motifs but more sparsely spaced out, or vice versa.

Movement

With pictorial papers it is generally clear in which direction the design should go – you don't want flamingos standing on their heads or upside-down flowerpots. But geometric or graphic designs and other abstract motifs allow you to play around with the sense of movement. Papers hung horizontally lower the ceiling visually and create a mood of stability. Vertically hung designs make rooms seem higher. Some patterns can even be hung on the diagonal, which creates a more active mood.

Detail

In period interiors the wall surface was broken down into segments defined by mouldings and trim, and different wall treatments were used for each section. At the top of the wall a frieze occupied the gap between the cornice and the picture rail. Below the picture rail the main wall area extended down to the dado rail, about two-thirds of the way down the wall. The lower portion of the wall occupied the area between the dado rail and the skirting board. Traditionally, each of these three distinct areas of wall was given a different treatment: the frieze may have been a decorative paper border, the main wall area was where the principal pattern was displayed, and the area below the dado rail was covered with a tougher paper or material that would resist wear and tear.

In contemporary interiors wallpaper is displayed flat, in a continuous plane, and without the proportional definition offered by mouldings and trim. Architectural detail may be minimal or absent altogether. In this situation, clean, crisp edges and adjacent surfaces in pristine condition are essential for the success of the look.

Photo murals – rather like the 'wallpapers' on computers – offer a window onto a whole new world, whether it's a beach scene, a Manhattan skyscape or a forest glade. Custom services are also available, enabling you to transform a favourite snapshot into wall art.

murals

Photographic murals provide a fresh spin on the old decorating standard of *trompe l'oeil*. Before the advent of such technology, you would have needed a seriously good painter to achieve anything capable of fooling the eye to this extent. Paper murals come in the form of wallpaper and are sold in rolls or panels. Some companies produce self-adhesive papers, which makes application easier. When you are hanging paper murals, there is next to no tolerance for error. Panels or rolls must be precisely matched so that they fit together seamlessly, otherwise the image will be out of joint.

material world

In the contemporary interior, materials speak for themselves. Smooth planes of plaster, expanses of polished wood, stone and tile complement the clean lines of modern design. Imports from industrial or commercial contexts, such as concrete, rubber, glass and steel, have also found widespread use in the home, as flooring, cladding, countertops and in a host of other applications. The interplay of different surfaces and finishes has played a crucial role in providing liveliness and character in otherwise restrained surroundings.

But what has been largely overlooked until now is that the material world has a softer side. Today textiles of all kinds, from furnishing fabric and rugs to lace and knitted materials, are back in the picture, delivering the essential dimension of comfort. Comfort on a physical level – textiles are warm and cushioning, and they help to keep sound

levels down. And comfort in an aesthetic sense, too – colour and pattern always delight the eye, wherever they crop up.

Because fabric has often been an important element in more conventional or traditional decorative styles, it's easy to forget that the twentieth century was a great period for contemporary textile design. Artists such as Raoul Dufy, Sonia Delaunay, Vanessa Bell and Duncan Grant created designs for fabric in the early decades of the century; in the post-war period there was an explosion of patterned textiles reflecting wide-ranging influences, from abstract art to scientific discoveries. A similar cross-fertilization can be seen today, blurring the boundaries of art, craft and product. New materials, new print technologies and a renewed interest in making things by hand has shaken up the home furnishings department like never before. Fabric is back, and once again it's at the cutting edge.

MATERIAL PATTERN BOOK

revival

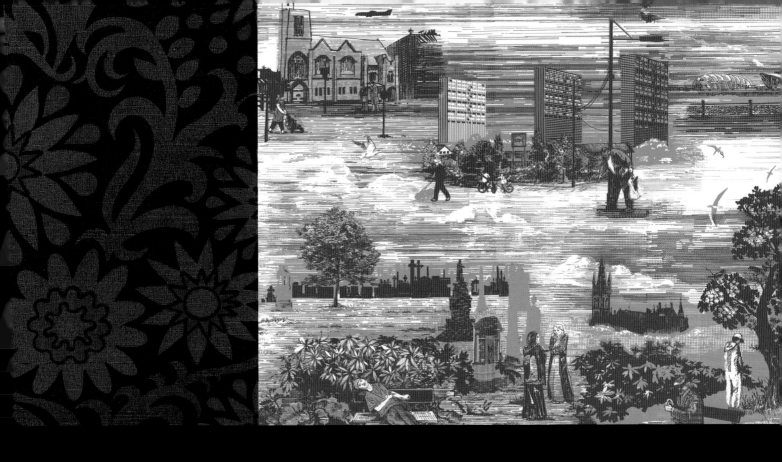

Printed fabrics have one great advantage over wallpaper, which is that they tend to be more enduring, meaning that original examples are more likely to be found in good condition. Unlike vintage wallpapers, which fade and discolour *in situ* and are prone to deterioration, there is still a reasonable stock of vintage fabric available from markets and other similar sources. As with papers, archive fabric designs are being reissued in new colourways and with motifs blown up in scale. Especially intriguing is the work of contemporary designers such as Timorous Beasties, whose subversion of the classic toile de Jouy features gritty urban scenes rather than bucolic landscapes.

MATERIAL PATTERN BOOK

graphic

Twentieth-century fabric design, particularly in the immediate post-war period, often featured graphic, stylized representations of natural forms, classic examples being designs produced by the renowned Finnish company Marimekko, particularly the work of Maija Isola. The innate cheerfulness of such patterns adds a lively, optimistic look to the interior, whether the fabric is used at the window or in the form of upholstery or cushion covers. Many such designs display a basic affinity that means they work well in mix-and-match combinations.

MATERIAL PATTERN BOOK

monochrome

The power of black and white patterning lies in its simplicity. Delivering maximum drama through minimum means, this traditional combination is as compelling as ever. Depending on the style of motif and imagery, monochromatic designs can suggest a baroque sophistication, the strength and boldness of geometric form or the subtlety of a pencil drawing. The inherent dominance of this type of pattern means that it demands plenty of breathing space. Plain coloured accents sing out in a black and white scheme; patterns, however, are less comfortable.

MATERIAL PATTERN BOOK

textured

Textured fabrics bring the subtle dimension of tactility into the material mix, creating an often welcome change of gear in schemes that are highly coloured or patterned. A recent revival of interest in handcrafted work, particularly knitting and crochet, has been given a new twist by the use of unusual materials – knitted and tufted strands of plastic, for example. Even lace has had a makeover. Computer technology has also been pressed into service to create intriguing tufted and looped textures, while laser-cutting delivers fine filigrees made of felt and leather.

mix and match

Textiles allow you to experiment with pattern on a relatively affordable scale. If you like to sew, knit or crochet, so much the better – woven fabrics aren't the only means of displaying colour and design. As with other printed or patterned surfaces, there are several approaches you can take. You can use a bold print to turn a chair or other upholstered piece into a focus of interest. You can opt for a coordinated look and use matching patterns in a range of applications. Or you can mix it all up to a greater or lesser degree.

*Change your cushion covers and update your interior in an instant. This is a great way to respond to decorative trends without breaking the bank. Or you can ring the changes with the seasons, swapping light summery prints for rich dark colours in the winter.

*Making cushion covers is a good way of using remnants or scraps of fabric salvaged from car boot sales, junk shops and other second-hand sources. You can also turn old curtains, bedspreads, tablecloths, tea towels or even dress material into cushion covers. If you haven't got enough fabric to cover the whole cushion, make the back of the cover out of another complementary pattern or a solid toning shade.

*Because cushions aren't subject to the same level of wear and tear as upholstered furniture, lighter fabrics can be brought into the mix – silk scarves, for example, or delicate handwoven textiles from far-flung corners of the world that you may have picked up while on holiday.

Mixing patterns

Mixing patterns successfully takes a bit of confidence and a good eye for colour. It's often a good idea to start small – with cushion covers, throws or similar details. You can always change the cover or move a cushion to a different location if the combination doesn't look right.

Big, small, geometric, floral, striped or spotty – you can mix many different patterns together provided that they all share some sort of basic affinity. It may be colour – patterns that display the same shades always work well together, even if the designs are very different in scale or type. Another useful common denominator is theme. Vintage prints from the same decade, for example, have a certain period look that makes them naturally harmonious in combination. Think about varying textures, too: knitted, tufted and embroidered materials add an extra dimension to the mix.

Matching patterns

The coordinated interior brings pattern to the forefront. Repeating the same design across several different elements – on the walls, at the windows, as bed linen or upholstery – creates a mood of intimacy and enclosure. The success of this strategy relies on wholeheartedness. Cover a sofa and armchairs in the same fabric and you're straying into three-piece suite territory. Extend the pattern or a version of the same pattern to walls and window treatments and you're making a strong decorative statement.

You've not only got to love pattern to go for this approach, you've got to absolutely adore the particular pattern you choose – because you'll be seeing a lot of it. The pattern will set the mood. When you're choosing designs and colourways, think about how you will use the room or area in question and what sort of atmosphere you want to create there – restful or lively, full of movement or more sedate. Flowing designs have a gentle rhythm that is conducive to relaxation. Symmetrical or geometric designs are more formal and orderly.

When you're using pattern on this scale, the quality of natural light that a room receives becomes an important factor. Get hold of a large sample of your chosen pattern, hang it up on the wall and live with it for a while to assess how it looks at different times of the day. In the northern hemisphere, the light in north-facing rooms is bluish and quite chilly. A pattern that features principal colours from the cool end of the spectrum will lower the visual temperature to freezing point. A south-facing aspect, on the other hand, has richer, warmer light. Cool colours in this situation can be refreshing and invigorating. A print that features warm dark colours will make a room seem more enclosed; cool airy colours push back the walls.

comfort zone

Expanses of smooth surfaces, minimal detailing and clean lines may define the modern interior, but that does not mean you have to reconcile yourself to a life of discomfort. Textiles and softer materials are what make homes livable. Upholstered furniture and piles of cushions in all shapes and sizes support the body in repose; soft furnishings offer scope for decorative flair – and a reason to be cheerful.

Upholstery options

Many upholstery fabrics are blends of natural and synthetic fibres. The synthetic component adds strength. Good upholstery materials are:

* Linen union – a blend of linen and cotton, linen union is more wear-resistant than either linen or cotton on its own.

* Tightly woven woollen fabrics (including tweed and suiting materials).

* Chenille – with a soft velvety texture, chenille is available in plain colours or patterns.

* Jacquard – a classic raised-pattern weave that takes its name from the loom on which it is produced.

* Velvet and moquette – moquette is similar to velvet, but has an uncut pile.

* Damask and brocade – these sumptuous materials typically feature a raised pattern as part of the weave.

* Leather and suede – leather ages especially well.

Using big prints

Large patterns can be very effective, even on small chairs or footstools – it is the scale of the design that really packs a punch and puts across a fresh approach. If you are using a big print, however, you need to think carefully about positioning. Ideally, the pattern should be centred so that no portion of the repeat is lost around the back. Either wrap the fabric around the chair to gauge the effect or take measurements along to the shop or outlet where you are buying the material so you can make sure the design will fit. Remember that when you are centring a large pattern you will need more fabric than if you were covering a chair or sofa in a smaller-scale design.

Loose or close-fitting?

The basic choice when it comes to upholstery styles is between loose covers and close-fitting or tailored upholstery. Loose covers are the more practical option because they can be removed for cleaning, which is an important consideration if there are children or pets in the household. They also provide an instant way of refreshing or updating a room, even on a seasonal basis. They are not a good choice, however, for contoured pieces of furniture – a sofa with a scrolled back, for example – or chairs with decorative legs that are meant to be seen. Loose covers do not sit well over sofas or chairs that are upholstered in textured materials such as velour or velvet.

If you are skilled at sewing, making loose covers is not difficult. Close-fitting upholstery tends to be a professional skill and can cost a significant amount, but it is a good way to revive a fundamentally sound piece that is looking past its best. If you are tempted to buy a second-hand chair or sofa with the intention of re-covering it, make sure there are no signs of woodworm or structural damage. Look for good strong shapes and classic lines.

Material considerations

Before you start thinking about specific designs and colours, you need to make sure you choose the right weight of fabric for the job it has to do. Upholstered furniture gets a fair bit of wear and lighter materials tend not to be suitable. If the fabric crumples when you gather it in your hand or if the cut edges fray easily, it's probably too lightweight to be used for upholstery. If you are in doubt, ask a sales assistant or an upholsterer for their advice.

Cushions covered in a number of different vintage fabrics make an attractive and harmonious display against the backdrop of a plain sofa. The designs, which are all floral, similar in style and date from the same period, go together perfectly. The striped rug introduces another patterned detail without being too insistent.

✳ Just because you own a Victorian chair, you don't have to cover it in a design that dates from the same period. Contrasts of style can be much more exciting. Cover a traditional chair or sofa with a bold contemporary print to update the look; cover a modern chair or sofa with a vintage pattern. Reupholstery is not cheap, but it is marginally less expensive than buying a new piece of furniture.

✳ Think about combining different prints and patterns on the same piece of furniture. Cover the arms in one fabric and the seat and back in another. Or cover the sides and back in one pattern and use a different pattern for the arms and seat – rather like a lining. It's generally more effective if the pattern used on the sides and back is more reticent than the one displayed at the front – a plain stripe that picks up one of the colours of the main fabric, for example.

❋Big is beautiful. Using large patterns turns chairs into objects of display. Covering a chair or sofa in a patterned material is a good way to experiment with a bolder decorative style if you are nervous about making a larger statement.

bedrooms

One place in the home where fabric has never gone out of fashion is the bedroom. Tactile bed linen made of crisp linen or the finest Egyptian cotton – or satin and silk if you're feeling really decadent – delivers comfort where it counts most: next to the skin. From stately tester beds hung with elaborate drapery to intimate boudoirs decked out in flounces and bows, fabric has also served as an important vehicle for expressing bedroom style over the ages. Today's bedrooms may be more tailored and clean-lined but the white-on-white purity of recent years has now given way to a bolder decorative look bursting with pattern and colour.

What the well-dressed bed is wearing

✽ Patterned bed linen – coordinated sets of duvet covers and pillowcases come in a wide range of contemporary designs, from sweet florals to polka dots, and graphic geometrics to bright tropical prints.

✽ Heaps of cushions – pillows and cushions covered in mix-and-match patterns and solid colours accessorize the bed and give a furnished look during the day – perfect if you're using the same space as a working or living area for part of the time.

✽ Upholstered headboards – simple padded panels covered with fabric provide an elegant and tailored finishing touch. Covering a headboard is a simple sewing project and a good way to display a stunning piece of material.

✽ Quilts, bedspreads throws and eiderdowns – add layers of sensuality with bedcovers made of embroidered silk, quilted satin, angora or cashmere.

Choosing bed linen

Synthetic materials and materials that contain a blend of synthetic and natural fibres may offer certain practical advantages – crease-resistance, for example – but nothing compares to pure natural fibres next to the skin. We spend about a third of our lives asleep – comfort in bed is a basic necessity, not a luxury.

The best natural fibres for bed linen are linen and cotton. Linen makes wonderful bed linen because it is absorbent and dries quickly, so you'll never feel clammy in bed. It's very strong and hard-wearing, and it's hypoallergenic and antistatic, too. With repeated washings, linen softens to a gorgeous texture. In the comfort stakes, cotton is a close runner-up. The finest cotton is Egyptian, which can be spun into very fine yarn that results in a silky, soft and hard-wearing woven fabric. Quality is also dependent on density (measured in threads per square inch): percale is a particularly smooth and densely woven cotton.

Putting the look together

When it comes to furniture, less is more in the bedroom. A bed is an extremely dominant piece of furniture because of its size. Unless your bedroom is vast, keep extraneous furniture to a minimum and either build in clothes storage or keep your wardrobe elsewhere. A room that is sparsely furnished provides more breathing space for decorative display in the form of colour and pattern.

❋ The bedroom is where we begin and end the day. Wake up to colours and patterns that make your heart sing. If you find all-over pattern too overwhelming, use cushions and pillowcases as a means of decorative display and keep walls and flooring plain.

❋ Strong patterns featuring dark colours can be very luxurious and moody in the bedroom. It's a more masculine look than rampaging florals and is well suited to a crisp, tailored approach.

❋ An upholstered bed, where the bed base as well as the headboard is covered in fabric, also provides the opportunity to inject strong colour into a decorative scheme.

windows

A window is a natural focal point in the interior – as a source of light and views, it draws the eye like a magnet. Plain blinds are worthy, but they are also dull. Curtains, drapery or panels of fabric in contemporary designs provide great scope for introducing the uplifting elements of colour and pattern. Lightweight or semi-transparent materials will filter the light in evocative ways.

Window dressing

Either full and gathered or hung in flat panels, fabric adds a softening element to the interior. The drape and hang of fabric also introduces a sense of movement that shutters, blinds and other solid window treatments lack, a quality that is further accentuated by pattern.

There's no limit to the effects you can create. In the contemporary interior, however, it's best to steer away from valances, pelmets and fussy detailing and let the fabric itself take centre stage. Similarly, elaborate poles, rails, finials and other accessories detract from the look. Keep it simple with plain rods or poles, or use concealed track.

What defines the style of a curtain or fabric window treatment is chiefly the heading. Simple gathered headings, where the material is shirred by means of a corded strip sewn on the reverse, are soft and pretty. Pleats are more formal. Ties or tab tops display fabric in flat panels. The choice of heading will determine the width of the curtain.

Another key variable is length. Choose sill-length or below-sill-length (apron-length) curtains for horizontal or strip windows, or in situations where full-length curtains would be impractical, such as in kitchens and bathrooms. Full-length curtains or drapery have more drama – just don't make the mistake of stopping the curtain at some indeterminate point between the sill and the floor, or they'll look as though they've shrunk.

You can use a much broader range of fabrics to make window treatments than you can use for upholstery, from lightweight sheer material for a filmy, gauzy effect to sumptuous velvets and brocades. Sheer materials diffuse the light and provide an element of privacy, making them a popular substitute for traditional net curtains. Multi- or double-track systems allow you to combine panels of sheer material in different colours for a layered look. Heavier fabrics require lining to hang properly and keep their shape.

❀ Gather a sample of your chosen fabric in your hand to assess how a heading will affect the appearance of the pattern. Simple gathers suit lightweight materials; heavier fabrics need more structured headings.

❀ When choosing fabric for window treatments, think about aftercare. Is the material shrink-proof? Can it be thrown in the washing machine or must it be dry-cleaned? Will it fade in sunlight? Silk is prone to fading and deteriorates quite quickly in strong light.

❀ Window treatments allow you to play around with the quality of light in the interior. Coloured sheers or semi-transparent fabrics tint the colour of the light – pinks, reds and oranges will warm up the light; blues and greens create a cooler effect.

❀ New printing technologies can transform windows into glowing backlit panels displaying digitally transferred imagery – a room with a view, day or night.

❀ Delicate effects reminiscent of lace panels or etched glass can be achieved by applying sheets of lace-cut acetate directly to windowpanes. Alternatively, copy out your favourite poem or prose passage in white paint to bring a whole new dimension to staring out of the window.

112
floors

The floor is the largest surface area after walls, and in contemporary open-plan layouts it can be a powerful unifying force. Flooring is undoubtedly an investment and many practical considerations must be taken into account when making a choice. But looks matter, too. Flooring materials that offer the bonus of colour and pattern provide a sense of vitality from the ground up and give spaces a strong identity.

Colour and pattern underfoot

Textiles such as carpets and rugs are not the only materials that deliver colour and pattern underfoot. For brilliant saturated colour, try rubber or vinyl, or paint wooden boards with glossy floor paint. Lino also comes in a wide range of colours, although shades are typically softer and slightly mottled. Sheet materials including lino and vinyl are available in a huge range of patterns for a seamless effect; alternatively, tiles, whatever the format and composition, are a patternmaker's dream.

✳ Prolong the life of floor textiles (carpets, natural-fibre coverings and rugs) by laying them over proper underlay. Nonslip matting is essential under rugs to prevent you from taking an unexpected trip on a flying carpet. Good-quality underlay provides extra cushioning, warmth and sound insulation, too.

✳ Some rugs are sold by the metre like carpeting, so it isn't difficult to get hold of a sample to take home and assess *in situ*. Some companies will also let you take full-size rugs home to try out before you commit yourself to a big purchase.

Floor-level art

Many floor coverings are permanent installations; at least, you certainly hope they will outlive a decorative scheme or two. That obviously poses certain limitations if you wake up one morning and fancy a change. Rugs, however, are a much more flexible way of providing floor-level interest. You can try them out in different locations, put them away when you're tired of them or want to clear the floor for a party, and take them with you when you move. A good rug will deliver years of delight, especially if it is well cared for.

Quality

There's nothing wrong with cheap mass-market buys if you're looking to inject a little instant pizzazz into your surroundings. Home furnishings departments stock a wide range of affordable contemporary rugs, ranging from flat-weaves like durries and kilims to tufted rugs featuring bold geometric designs. Texture, density and fibre content affect how well a rug will wear. Long or shaggy pile is best restricted to bedrooms and areas of light traffic. For hallways and other circulation areas, you're better off choosing denser woven wool rugs that can take the punishment.

At the upper end of the market, rugs get seriously expensive. The most prized are handwoven or hand-knotted rugs. While prices are steep, such high-quality rugs are an investment and should increase in value over the years – and they will last for ever. Companies specializing in contemporary rugs sell designs by famous names that are true works of art. Some rug designs from the early modernist period are still in production. When you're choosing a rug of this quality, follow your heart and opt for whatever sends your pulse racing. You can always base the rest of your decor around it.

Placement

Rugs are good spatial unifiers. A centrally positioned rug draws a seating area together; under a dining table it defines an eating area. It's best to suit the size and shape of the rug to the area in question: too small and it will look like a postage stamp; too big and you'll lose a lot of it under furniture. Round rugs can introduce a new dynamic in a space that is severely rectilinear. Spotty or stripy runners in bright colours are fantastically welcoming in halls and on stairs – like a vibrant thread connecting areas together.

objects
of desire

It's no longer necessary to stick to the straight and narrow when it comes to furnishing the contemporary home. Old and new, classic and contemporary work well together when handled with confidence and flair – good news for those who have vintage treasures lurking in the attic or whose idea of shopping is a trawl around salvage yards, antique shops, markets and second-hand stalls. When you catch sight of that must-have item and your heart skips a beat, don't waste too much time thinking about whether it will fit (except in the physical sense, of course). The only style that counts is your own.

Objects of desire come in all shapes and sizes. It may be today's statement lights that send your pulse racing, or

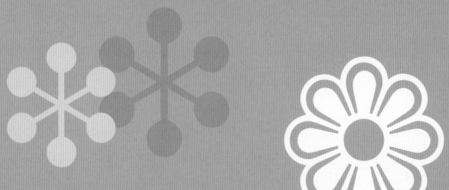

great designs from the twentieth century such as Eames or Panton chairs. Perhaps you find yourself irresistibly drawn to patterned china the way some people are to shoes – you can never have enough. Whatever you're fixed upon, display it prominently and enjoy it.

A home full of character and meaning can't be assembled overnight like a kit of parts, or ordered from a catalogue down to the last detail. Part of the joy is bringing new discoveries to the mix – adding a bit here, subtracting a little there. Our lives don't stand still and there's no reason why our homes should be static, either. Change is what keeps our surroundings full of vitality and makes them a true source of pleasure.

lighting

Contemporary lighting used to be all about discreet, functional fittings carefully positioned to turn walls and ceilings into glowing planes of light. While such an approach retains its merits, it ignores one of the key elements of lighting, which is sheer theatricality. Recently, however, there has been a huge shift in lighting design and a host of intriguing

and exuberant fittings have appeared on the market that more than redress the balance. It would be exhausting if every single light in your home was a show stopper, but there's nothing like a statement light to inject instant glamour and allure.

Chandeliers can be hung almost anywhere – bedrooms and kitchens, as well as living rooms and dining areas. But they need plenty of breathing space, especially those that are on a larger scale. Double-height rooms or stairwells can also be good places to showcase this type of decorative light.

Think about height: if you hang a chandelier too close to the ceiling, its impact will be wasted; too low down and it will interrupt views.

Some chandeliers are seriously heavy and may require additional support.

Any light fitting that features multiple points of light introduces a mood of festivity and celebration. Fairy lights have become ubiquitous in many homes, wound around headboards or handrails, or trailing along mantelpieces. Taking this one step further, some new light designs take the form of asymmetric floral branches covered in twinkling LEDs that are designed to be displayed flat against the wall.

Points of light

The chandelier is back – and how it's changed. One of the most popular decorative lights for centuries, the chandelier is essentially a branched fitting featuring multiple points of light. Its particular attraction is the fact that it provides a focus of interest whether it is lit or not. In traditional designs, tiers of faceted glass or crystal beads and drops fracture the light and create a glittering ensemble that dazzles the eye. In the hands of modern designers, the same basic form has been reinterpreted, often very wittily – the tiers of crystal replaced by magnifying lenses, transparent film canisters, cascading wine glasses and other sideways leaps of the creative imagination. New technology has also proved a fruitful source of inspiration, with some designers weaving chandeliers out of delicate fronds of fibre optics.

Decorative light

✳ Decorative lights may not contribute much to overall levels of illumination but they do bring immense charm and artistic flair to the interior. Sculptural designs marry form with light to create lit objects or furniture. One of the classic modern examples is Tom Dixon's Jack light, a seat that lights up or a light you can sit on, whichever way you like to think of it. Similar is the Lace Cube (above right) by McCollin Bryan, a clear cast resin table that is lit from inside.

✳ Another variation on the theme of the chandelier is Light Shade Shade by Jurgen Bey and Droog Design. A cylinder of semi-transparent mirror film surrounds a traditional chandelier. The chandelier is visible only when the light is switched on.

✳ Project images onto walls and ceilings for your own light show. Sophisticated programmable systems are now available that allow you to vary colour, pattern, image and tempo to create a true indoor spectacle. What better way of livening up plain white walls?

The hottest antiques on the market today aren't that old – middle-aged, at best. Collectors have woken up to the potential of mid-century modern, not merely as investment pieces but as furniture to live with and enjoy. The line between vintage and retro has always been blurred, but with designs from the 1960s and 1970s becoming increasingly desirable, the past is fast catching up with us. Original pieces in mint condition are rare, but many designs from the greatest twentieth-century names such as Eames, Panton, Saarinen and Jacobsen remain in production. Good design always looks great.

21st-century collectables

Collectable vintage furniture holds its value. If you wake up one morning and feel like ditching your 1950s pieces in favour of a 1970s look, provided that you've kept the furniture in good condition, you stand a fair chance of making your money back when you sell. If you're on a budget and can't afford the real thing, look out for convincing knock-offs or lookalikes.

Mix and match

Some people fall in love with a particular period of design and go to great lengths to furnish their home accordingly, right down to the very last detail. But not everyone wants to live in a time warp. Mixing modern and vintage gives an interior a grounded look without turning the clock back several decades every time you open the front door. Pair a sleek up-to-the-minute light fitting with a reclaimed metal desk, or a cutting-edge kitchen with a retro dining table and chairs, and you can have the best of both worlds. Vintage furniture that's seen a bit of life has patina and character, which bring depth to the mix.

130

Collecting

✿ One of the keys to successful collecting is to make it personal and buy the things that you really like. For lovers of vintage, the fun is in the search – it's so much more satisfying to stumble across a new find than to have it all laid out for you in a carefully styled room set.

✿ If you're serious about collecting for investment potential, do your homework. Read up on the period or designer that interests you. Condition is all-important, and so is provenance. In many cases it's not merely the designer's name that counts, it's also the manufacturer. Many contemporary classics have had a chequered history of production, with designs being produced under licence by different companies at different times. The most expensive and rarest pieces are early first editions or prototypes.

✿ The Internet – eBay in particular – has really exploded the market for contemporary classics. Other sources worth checking out include furniture companies manufacturing classic designs under licence, auction houses (even the big names are in on the act), dealers specializing in twentieth-century furniture, junk shops, markets and car boot sales. It's worth searching in country districts away from major cities where the market is more clued-up.

Buying vintage doesn't have to cost the earth, although as more people become design-aware, prices will undoubtedly continue to rise. Some companies, such as Habitat, have made it their policy to reissue design standards at affordable prices. Robin Day's moulded plastic chair, for example – the ubiquitous utility seating of every doctor's waiting room and school hall – was given a new lease of life in recent years when it was reissued in a lighter, translucent polypropylene and a range of upbeat colours. The trend for collecting modern furniture has also given up-and-coming design talent a welcome boost. Keep an eye out for interesting new work and you could find yourself owning a future classic.

details

Those who decorate and furnish their home with an eye on resale value tend to make safe, predicable choices that won't upset anyone. But if you don't express your personality in your own surroundings, you might as well be living in a hotel. Detail is the foreground of the picture, a chance to make a statement about what you really like and what really moves you.

Room for display

You don't have to be a photographer's
stylist to create effective decorative
displays. Nor is it about showing off
expensive purchases or advertising your
perfect taste. What counts is your sense
of delight in what you choose to put on
show, however ephemeral or inexpensive
that may be. Displays of decorative
objects, like fashion accessories, allow
you to respond to new directions in design
without committing yourself to a complete
stylistic overhaul. At the same time, a
display doesn't have to be set in stone,
assuming squatter's rights on a shelf,
mantelpiece or wall for years on end.
Swap things around from time to time to
give your eye something fresh to look at.

Collections – of patterned plates,
vintage containers, framed photographs
or retro mirrors – always look best if they
are grouped together in a single location
where they will read as a coherent entity.
Group them by colour or theme, provide
plenty of surrounding breathing space,
and allow room for future acquisitions.

Digital transfer

Cutting-edge print technology enables you to display an image in a new and unexpected medium, and give your home a truly individual touch. Images can be transferred digitally to many different surfaces and materials, including fabric, tile and laminate, as well as paper, broadening the scope considerably. While such technology was first exploited commercially on small accessories and jokey gift products, such as mugs, mouse mats, handbags, T-shirts and place mats, large-scale applications are now available, which have much more decorative impact.

Design gallery

Many companies specializing in digital printing have their own extensive image banks, so you can choose a design to suit both your interior and the particular application that you have in mind. Images typically include abstract patterns, natural forms such as flower heads and seed pods, travel scenes, architectural details and other more kitsch or pop art designs. You can often specify a different colourway or customize an image with a special effect.

*If you want to use your own image – a family snapshot, for example – as the basis of a printed design, it needs to be the best possible quality, whatever format it comes in. Photographs should be no smaller than A5 (15 x 20cm/6 x 8in); digital images should be high resolution (no less than 300 dpi – dots per inch).

*Four-colour images can be reproduced in four-colour, black and white, sepia or in any other shade you wish.

*Remember that the larger your image is blown up, the greater the pixelation.

Digitally printed fabric lends itself to a wide range of applications, including bespoke bed linen, cushions and curtains. Striking Roman or roller blinds, which hang flat against the window, are a great way of displaying family photographs. The effect is enhanced by backlighting.

Upholstered furniture is another way of turning a print into a decorative display. The blown-up scale and photographic clarity of the print is what gives such applications their immense impact. Some companies produce a range of basic furniture, such as chairs, chaise longues, footstools and floor cushions, which they will upholster with the design of your choice.

Other uses of digital prints are as wall hangings or panels. Images can be printed directly onto canvases of varying sizes and can even be split into several sections – or you could supply a series of freeze-frames and have them printed up individually to introduce a sense of movement to your display.

practicalities

planning the work

This section covers various aspects of the practical side of decorating, so that you can tackle the work with confidence yourself or commission others in an informed way. Basic painting and simple sewing projects fall within most people's capabilities; other jobs, especially those involving lighting and electrical work, should most definitely be left to the professionals.

DIY or professional?

The first step is to decide how much of the work you are going to do yourself and whether there are any aspects of your proposed decorative scheme that will need professional input. Factors to consider include:

❋ *Your skills level* If you're a practical, hands-on sort of person, many decorative tasks will not pose too great a challenge, even if you haven't tackled a particular job before. But if you're all thumbs and lack patience, it's best to call someone in to do the work for you. Don't talk yourself into the DIY route simply as a means of saving money – you may find yourself spending more in the long run if you make a mess of things.

❋ *Job satisfaction* If you derive satisfaction from accomplishing tasks about the home, you are a better candidate for DIY than someone who finds such work a chore. Some people find DIY relaxing. If you simply hate it, however, you are more likely to skimp and cut corners, which will lead to a poor result.

❋ *Budget* Your time costs money, too.

❋ *Scheduling* Have you got enough free time to complete all stages of the work to a satisfactory standard? Half-completed projects that hang on weekend after weekend often stay that way.

❋ *Health and safety* Make sure you know your limitations. A few hours up a ladder decorating a ceiling can give you strained muscles and back pain if you're not used to it. Electrical work must always be carried out by a qualified professional.

❋ *Cost of materials* Consider commissioning the work if the job involves expensive materials that you might damage through inexperience.

❋ *Teamwork* Can you call on a partner or friend for assistance? DIY teams make jobs quicker and more pleasant.

Budgeting

Set a budget for decoration before you begin so you don't find yourself overspending some way down the line. Work out what you can afford, then research the market to see what this will buy you in terms of materials and/or assistance.

❋ Account for everything – the cost of preparation, tools and materials, final finishes, hardware, professional help, and so on. You may need to hire specialist tools, for example, to sand a floor. If you're making curtains, add the cost of track or poles, heading tape and lining to the cost of fabric.

❋ Add in a margin of about 10 per cent for contingency. This gives you an allowance to fall back on if things don't turn out as planned.

❋ Think about how long you expect decoration to remain in place. Do you intend to remain in your home for the near future?

❋ Consider ongoing maintenance costs. Are there special seals that will need to be renewed? Will fabric require regular dry-cleaning?

❋ If your preferred option looks too expensive, take a sideways step and reconsider your plans. Using cheaper materials can be a false economy.

Hiring professionals

Professionals specializing in decoration cover a wide range of trades, from plasterers to painters, curtain-makers to floor-layers. Some may have expertise in handling a particular material, such as stone. If you require something very specific, it's best not to rely on an all-rounder.

❋ Do your research. Word of mouth is often the best route, so ask friends who have had similar work done for their recommendations. Many retailers and department stores keep professional fitters/makers on their books. Otherwise, follow up articles in magazines and local newspapers or look for accredited professionals in the Yellow Pages.

❋ If the work is more involved than a straightforward paint job, for example, ask for references and take them up.

❋ Ask for an estimate of cost before you agree to hire someone. You may wish to get several quotes for a price comparison. Don't necessarily opt for the person who puts in the lowest quote.

❋ Hire professionals who are members of accredited trade associations or similar bodies. This allows you to take up a complaint with the body in question should things go wrong and perhaps gain some redress.

❋ Be specific about what you want. The clearer and more detailed you can be in your briefing, the more likely you are to get what you want.

❋ Put everything in writing and keep all receipts and delivery notes.

❋ Try to resist changing your mind once work is under way. Costs escalate and jobs overrun when there are frequent changes of tack.

❋ Never pay upfront. A small float for materials is OK at the start of the job, but the lion's share of the fee should be handed over only on satisfactory completion of the work.

❋ Plan ahead and be prepared to wait. Good professionals are generally booked up into the future. Don't be tempted to take on someone who isn't up to the job in your haste to get the work done quickly. Ask for an indication of how long the job will take and get a firm start date.

Work on site

If the job entails work on site, as many decorative projects do, establish at the outset what sort of disruption you can expect and how long it will last.

❋ Agree where tools and materials will be stored overnight.

❋ Some jobs are messier than others. Any work that involves sanding or replastering, for example, will generate dust and mess. Make it clear that you expect your home to be left tidy at the end of the day, but don't insist on unreasonable standards of cleanliness until the messy stage is over.

❋ Don't interfere or hover over your decorator's shoulder. Inspect the work at the end of the day and raise any queries then. But remain on hand to make decisions if necessary.

❋ Allow reasonable access to kitchen and bathroom facilities.

❋ Before work begins, remove breakable or valuable items from the area.

preparing surfaces for decoration

The standard decorative treatments for walls include painting, papering and tiling. The best results in each case require careful preparation of the surfaces beforehand. Preparation takes up the greater part of any decorative work on walls – final finishes are just the tip of the iceberg. If you've ever watched a professional painter at work, for example, you will have noticed how much time is spent on making the underlying surface as good as possible. Careful preparation makes all the difference between a passable result and a good one.

Preparing painted or plastered walls

✳ Clear the room or area in question of all breakable and valuable items. Remove as much of the furniture as you can and group the remainder to one side or in the centre of the space, so that it can be fully covered with dustsheets or protective polythene sheeting. If possible, cover the entire floor area with drop cloths or sheeting to protect it from splashes, drips and spills. If you don't, you may track wet paint or paste into unprotected areas.

✳ Brush or vacuum the walls and ceiling to remove cobwebs, surface dirt and loose debris.

✳ Examine the surface for cracks, holes, bumps, dents and other imperfections and fill these with a proprietary filler using a pliable putty or palette knife. Allow the patches to dry, sand down and fill again. Filler shrinks as it dries, so you may need to repeat the process several times until the wall is smooth and even.

✳ Wash down the walls with warm water and a mild nonabrasive, nonfoaming detergent to remove grease and grime as well as any residue from sanding.

✳ Seriously battered, uneven walls call for greater intervention. You may need to hire a plasterer to give the wall a skim coat to even out any bumps and irregularities. Alternatively, you can have the wall cross-lined with lining paper – papering horizontally and then vertically will give you a smooth surface to work on.

Woodwork and trim

Whatever final finish you are planning for your walls – paint or paper – you should prepare the woodwork (doors, door frames and skirting boards) and any other decorative trim or mouldings before you go on to the next stage.

✳ It is not uncommon for trim, moulding or cornicing to become clogged up with successive layers of paint. Use chemical strippers or a blowtorch to restore crispness – although this is arduous, time-consuming work, sharp detailing sets off final finishes to perfection. Work into small crevices using an old toothbrush or similar tool.

✳ Fill any cracks and holes in trim using an appropriate filler and, when dry, sand smooth.

✳ Lightly sand gloss finishes to provide a key for repainting.

✳ After sanding, always wipe down with a damp cloth to remove any dust or other residue.

Stripping wallpaper

Stripping wallpaper is not a job for the faint-hearted. It takes plenty of patience and elbow grease, as well as specialist tools. There are several methods you can use, depending on the type of paper you are stripping. These include soaking and scraping, steam stripping and chemical stripping. Always protect the floor with a waterproof polythene dustsheet and cover those furnishings you can't remove. Walls that are covered with layers of paper, with painted paper or with heavy or embossed paper will take more work to strip.

BASIC STRIPPING

✳ Score lines in the paper using a scoring tool. Don't press too hard or you will damage the underlying plaster.

✳ Fill a bucket with hot water and add a little washing-up liquid. Use a sponge to wet the paper with the solution and leave it to soak in for half an hour. Repeat the process, making sure the water is hot.

✳ Use a wallpaper scraper to ease the paper from the wall.

STEAM STRIPPING

✳ Score the paper as described above.

✳ Use a steam stripper to dissolve the wallpaper paste. After you fill the stripper with water, it is heated by an element to boiling point, whereupon steam issues from a flat plate that you hold to the wall.

✳ Once the paper has loosened, scrape it from the wall.

PROPRIETARY SYSTEMS

There are a number of proprietary products on the market, ranging from chemical strippers to systems that involve applying sheets of paper that have been soaked in a chemical solution to the wall, to help dissolve the paste.

VINYL PAPERS

New vinyl papers are designed so that the surface peels off easily, leaving a porous backing paper on the wall. This can be removed by spraying with a dissolving solution and scraping off with a skimmer tool.

Safety

Preparing surfaces can be messy and dusty. Wear appropriate old clothes and shoes. Wear rubber gloves if you are handling chemicals. Protect your eyes from flecks of paint by wearing safety goggles. You may need to wear a face mask if the work is generating a lot of dust. Make sure that any ladders that you use are robust and stable; don't attempt to reach high places by standing on tables or chairs.

painting walls and ceilings

Most people can make a decent job of painting, provided that they take the time to prepare the surface properly beforehand. The next stage is to apply one or more undercoats or primer to seal the surface and provide a neutral base for overpainting in the final colour.

Types of paint

❋*Undercoat or primer* This seals bare plaster and covers dark or strong colours. Apply a second coat if the underlying colour still shows through after the first coat has dried. Primers are oil-based, which means tools and brushes must be cleaned in white spirit, which needs to be disposed of responsibly. If your top coat is an emulsion paint, however, you can use diluted white (water-based) emulsion as an undercoat.

❋*Emulsion paint* Water-based paint that is available in a huge range of colours. Easy to work with and quick-drying. Clean brushes and tools with water and a little detergent.

❋*Eggshell paint* Also known as semi-gloss, mid-sheen, silk or satin. Oil-based paints are more durable and are best used on woodwork and doors. Eggshell paint takes longer to dry than emulsion. Clean tools with white spirit.

❋*Gloss paint* This dries to a high shine and is very durable. Use on woodwork or doors, or metalwork. Clean tools with white spirit.

❋*Kitchen and bathroom paint* Water-based paint that is formulated to absorb moisture in steamy locations, and contains fungicides.

❋*Specialist or historic paint finishes* Limewash, distemper and many other traditional paints are available from specialist suppliers. These are slightly more difficult to apply than conventional paints. Some types need to be painted on a wall that has been stripped of all modern emulsions.

❋*Eco paints* Specially formulated to be kind to the environment. The range of colours available and ease of application have greatly improved in recent years.

How much paint?

Average coverage is indicated on most paint tins. Bear in mind that some surfaces are more absorbent than others; highly coloured or textured surfaces will also require more coats. Calculate the area you need to cover by breaking the surface down into self-contained rectangles and multiplying height by width. Always err on the generous side: it may be difficult to colour-match exactly if you run out of paint before you finish and it is always useful to keep a supply on hand for retouching at a later date.

Painting tools

Buy the best-quality tools you can afford. Cheap brushes shed hairs and give a streaky finish; cheap rollers deteriorate and crumble. The best brushes are made of real bristle; the best rollers from natural fibres such as lambswool. Clean tools thoroughly after use. If you are leaving the job for an hour or so, you can wrap brushes or rollers in foil, plastic film or a plastic bag to prevent them from drying out.

❋*Brushes* Equip yourself with a selection of sizes. Small widths (25mm and 50mm) are useful for trim; large widths (100mm or 150mm) are good for walls and ceilings. Angled 'cutting-in' brushes allow you to paint corners or window frames with ease.

❋*Rollers* Recommended for use with emulsion paint only. Rollers speed up painting, but they tend to produce a slight 'orange peel' texture, which some people find less appealing. Use in combination with a paint tray.

❋*Paint kettle* A container with a handle for decanting small amounts of paint from large tins.

❋*Paint shield* This is a plastic or metal shield that prevents you from overpainting onto glass or the floor.

Basic painting techniques

Painting isn't difficult but there is an art to achieving a smooth, even coverage. Work in discrete sections that you can complete in the time you have available: don't stop midway along a wall. Never attempt to rush a job by applying paint too thickly.

❋*Applying emulsion with a brush* Work in horizontal bands of about 60cm, starting at the top of the wall and moving down as each band is complete. Brush on the paint in all directions, then lay off the paint when the brush is slightly dry, using cross-strokes and finishing with an upward flick.

❋*Applying emulsion with a roller* Fill a third of the tray with paint, dip the roller in the reservoir and run it over the ridged section to spread the paint over the roller. Use a steady, gentle, even pressure to roller the paint back and forth on the wall in diagonal strokes. As the roller dries, finish by smoothing the painted area in straight upward lines.

❋*Applying oil-based paint with a brush* Work from the top. Paint three vertical stripes next to each other, leaving a gap just narrower than the brush. As the paint runs out, brush across the stripes to fill the gaps, working top to bottom. Always work to a wet edge.

Order of painting

❋Start with the ceiling. Paint in strips, working away from the main source of natural light.

❋Paint the walls next. Start at a corner and work in 60cm bands or blocks from the top to the bottom.

❋Finally, paint the woodwork, window frames and doors. Use an appropriate width of brush for the area you are painting. Paint flush doors from top to bottom, tackling the frame last. For a panelled door, paint the panels first, top to bottom, then the frame. Paint mouldings next to glazing before painting the frames.

papering walls

Papering demands rather more skill than painting and mistakes can be costly to rectify. The most expensive papers, including hand-blocked designs, are the hardest to hang and it is generally advisable to call in a professional to tackle the job. Large-scale repeats also demand a certain degree of expertise.

Paper and paste

Measure the height and perimeter of your room, including the widths of standard doors and windows, but excluding large openings, such as French doors. Then refer to charts (published in pattern books, provided by the store or supplier, or available on the Internet) to calculate how many rolls of wallpaper you will need. Widths of paper vary, according to country of origin. You will need more rolls if the motif is very large; some companies allow you to return unused (and unopened) rolls. Make sure that all rolls come from the same batch to avoid colour variation.

Use the brand of paste recommended by your wallpaper supplier. Heavier papers need stronger adhesion. Most papers (except vinyl) need to rest for a short period of 10 to 15 minutes after pasting to allow for expansion, so that they do not expand once they are hung on the wall and distort the pattern alignment.

How to paper a wall

✳ Prepare the walls as described previously (see page 143). For best results, cover the walls in lining paper and paint the ceiling first.

✳ Equip yourself with a folding pasting table about 1.8m long, a paste brush, bucket (or water tray if the paper is pre-pasted), long scissors, trimming knife, seam roller, plumb line and bob or carpenter's level, sponge and wide (250mm) paperhanger's brush.

✳ Begin papering on a wall next to the main window and work away from the direction of the light so that joins are less noticeable. However, if the paper features a large design, centre the first sheet in the middle of the wall and work towards the corners where interruptions in the design will be less noticeable.

✳ Draw a vertical line one roll's width out from the corner, less 1cm for turning the corner. Use a carpenter's level or plumb line and bob.

✳ Apply a coat of size to the wall, so that the paper can be slid into place. You can either use diluted wallpaper paste or buy special size from a supplier.

✳ Make up the paste according to instructions.

✳ Unroll the wallpaper on the pasting table, pattern side down, and cut the first drop to length, allowing an extra 100mm for trimming.

✳ Turn the paper over. Unroll the next length and match the pattern edge to edge. Cut several drops to size in the same way, numbering each on the back in the correct order.

✳ Place the first drop pattern side down on the pasting table and brush out a light coat of paste, working from the centre of the paper outwards. Wipe off any paste that gets onto the table (or anywhere else) immediately using a sponge.

✳ Fold or 'book' the wallpaper. Gently fold the top half down to the middle, pasted side facing pasted side, and then fold the bottom half up to the middle, pasted side facing pasted side as before. Make a note of which is the top end of the drop.

✳ Leave the paper to expand for the recommended time.

✳ Hang the first drop, aligning the outer edge with the pencil line and leaving an excess of 50mm at the top for trimming. Gently smooth the paper against the wall using your hand or a brush, working inwards towards the corner. Release the top half of the paper and smooth it out, working from the centre outwards.

✳ Release the lower fold and smooth it into place as before. Inspect for any wrinkles or air bubbles. If a bubble won't be smoothed over, prick it with a pin to release the air before the paper is dry.

✳ Crease the paper at the top and bottom edge, and trim it to fit.

✳ Follow the same procedure to hang the next strips, making sure the pattern is correctly aligned.

✳ After you have hung a few drops, go over the joins with a seam roller to ensure a neat finish.

✳ To paper around corners, measure the distance between the last full width and the corner, adding 13mm for an overlap, and cut a drop to this width. Paste it and hang it, as before. Use the offcut as the first drop on the adjoining wall. Measure the width of the offcut and draw a vertical line down the wall the same distance from the corner, using a plumb line and bob or carpenter's level. Align the right edge of the offcut with this line.

✳ To paper around a light switch, turn off the electricity at the mains and unscrew the switch cover. Paper down as far as the switch, pierce the paper over the centre of the switch and cut the paper diagonally to reveal it; trim the flaps and slip the switch cover through the hole. Then hang the rest of the drop and screw the cover back into place.

✳ To wallpaper around windows and doors, hang a strip and smooth it into place against the frame of the door or window. Then make a diagonal cut at the corner of the frame and trim around the frame with a trimming knife.

soft furnishings

You don't have to be particularly skilled at needlework to experiment creatively with fabric. Small-scale projects, such as making cushion covers, tablecloths and simple window drapery, may require very little in the way of sewing. Once you have built up your confidence, you can go on to more complicated and challenging items. For most people, however, ambitious soft-furnishing projects, such as reupholstery and fully tailored curtains, will always remain jobs for a professional. If you are unsure of your ability to tackle a project, it is always worth spending a little extra and enlisting the help of a professional maker.

Types of fabric

When choosing fabric, it's important to check that the weight and type of fabric are suitable for the particular use you have in mind. Make a note of its composition, the type of cleaning and maintenance that is recommended, and whether it is shrink- or fade-resistant. Colours vary from batch to batch, so always buy enough fabric to complete the job.

✳ *Acetate* An artificial fibre with similar qualities to silk, but less likely to rot or fade. Use it as a stand-in for silk.

✳ *Brocade* Luxurious woven fabric, with a raised (jacquard) design and opulent appearance, made of silk, wool, cotton or blends.

✳ *Cambric* Closely woven cotton or linen, with a sheen on one side.

✳ *Canvas* A coarse cotton or cotton and linen blend that comes in different widths and is suitable for blinds.

✳ *Chintz* Traditional cotton furnishing fabric, typically printed with floral patterns or birds. Unglazed chintz is called cretonne. Glazed chintz has a resin coating on one side that gives a soft sheen and repels dust.

✳ *Cotton* A versatile fibre that can be readily dyed and printed. It can be finished in different ways or blended with artificial fibres. Cotton duck is a heavy weave that is suitable for no-sew curtains. Cotton lawn is smooth and fine.

✳ *Damask* Woven fabric, similar to brocade, with a jacquard design, although the relief pattern is smoother and the fabric is reversible. Composition varies: silk, linen, cotton, rayon or blends.

✳ *Dupion* Originally imported Indian silk, it is now often made from viscose and acetate.

✳ *Gingham* Cheap, fresh cotton fabric with a checkered pattern (a single colour on white).

✳ *Holland* Medium-weight fabric in cotton or linen, often used for roller blinds as it does not fray.

✳ *Lace* Delicate openwork fabric, traditionally handmade from linen threads. Handmade or heirloom lace is very expensive; much cheaper is machine-made lace in cotton or blends.

✳ *Linen* A natural fibre made from flax, available in different weaves and finishes. Linen is very strong but creases easily. Linen union is a hard-wearing blend of linen and cotton.

✳ *Moire* Silk fabric with a watered or wavy pattern; synthetic moire is made of acetate.

✳ *Muslin* Light, strong, cheap and sheer cotton fabric, usually white or off-white. Suitable for sheers and drapery.

✳ *Organdie* Very light, strong, sheer cotton, treated to enhance stiffness and crispness.

✳ *Polyester* Artificial fabric that hangs well, often used in cotton blends to reduce creasing.

✳ *Sateen* Strong cotton or cotton-blend fabric with a dull sheen; this often comes in solid colours.

✳ *Satin* Fabric with a strong sheen on one side. Silk satin is expensive; cotton satins are more affordable and practical.

✳ *Silk* The most luxurious traditional furnishing fabric, made from the fibres of silkworm cocoons. Silk dyes very well and is soft and strong, but it is expensive and rots when exposed to sunlight.

✳ *Taffeta* This is a stiffer form of silk or artificial silk, and is smooth and shiny on both sides.

✳ *Ticking* Striped cotton fabric traditionally used to cover mattresses, usually with narrow black or blue stripes on a white ground. This is a very sturdy and hard-wearing fabric.

✳ *Velvet* Fabric with a dense, smooth pile on one side, which may be made of silk, cotton, polyester or rayon.

✳ *Viscose* An artificial fibre with a soft sheen, often used in blends with cotton and silk.

✳ *Voile* Thin, soft and sheer fabric, often made of polyester.

Making a basic square cushion

This method, which requires minimal sewing skills, can be adapted to make covers for square cushions of any size. In addition to fabric, you will need a cushion pad. If you want the cushion cover to be removable for washing, you will also need some simple means of closure, either ribbons, ties or buttons.

✳ Calculate the amount of fabric required by measuring the width of the cushion pad across the middle from seam to seam, adding a seam allowance of 3cm (1.5cm for each seam). To make a plump cushion, make the cover 2.5cm smaller than the pad.

✳ Cut out two pieces of fabric to the right dimensions, place them with right sides facing and pin together along the seam allowance on all four sides of the cover.

✳Stitch along three sides of the cover, leaving an opening on one side so that the pad can be inserted. Sewing can be done by hand, but machine-stitching will be stronger.

✳If you would like the cover to be removable, hem each side of the opening and attach fabric ties or ribbons. Alternatively, you can sew buttons in place and secure the closure with fabric loops. If you don't mind that the cover cannot be removed, you can sew the opening closed once the cushion pad is inside.

✳Turn the cover so that the right sides are facing out and fill it with the cushion pad.

✳Either tie the ties or ribbons, button the cover up, or simply turn over the edges of the opening and neatly stitch it closed.

Windows and blinds

Window treatments vary in style from simple clip-on drapery or roller blinds to fully lined formal curtains with pleated or gathered headings. There are many different variables to consider, from style of heading and choice of hardware to preferred length. Decide on the effect you're after first, because this will have a direct bearing on the quantity of fabric that you'll need.

MEASURING WINDOWS

Whether you are making a window treatment yourself or commissioning a professional to make blinds or curtains for you, taking accurate measurements is essential.

✳Would you prefer the treatment to hang inside the window frame or overlap it?

✳If you have decided on curtains, how long do you want them to be? How wide? Do you want them to draw clear of the window or overhang it by a margin on either side?

✳The length or 'drop' of a curtain will depend on the type of hardware or suspension system you choose. A thin pole, for example, will give a different drop from a thick, chunky one. If you are using a pole, calculate the length from the bottom of the rings, not from the pole itself.

✳Equip yourself with a steel tape measure. Don't use cloth tapes because they stretch out of shape and are not accurate. Enlist a helper, particularly if you are measuring windows that are very long or very wide and you need to use a stepladder.

✳Choose one system of measurement, metric or imperial, and stick to it. Take all measurements at least twice.

✳If you are measuring a pair of windows, don't assume they are the same size. Measure each one individually.

✳For treatments that will hang inside the window frame or recess, measure the width at the top, middle and bottom of the window, and choose the narrowest measure as the final width.

✳For treatments that will hang outside the window frame, allow for 5cm clearance on either side (in other words, add 10cm to the width) and allow for 10cm clearance above the frame (which will add 10cm to the overall drop).

✳Roman blinds need extra clearance at the top. Add 20cm to the overall drop.

✳If you want draperies to overlap in the middle, add an extra 8cm to each curtain or panel.

✳If you will need to join panels to make the required fullness, don't forget to add in a seam allowance.

✳To calculate length, take two measurements from top to bottom and choose the shortest as the final length.

✳For sill-length curtains, measure to 1cm above the sill.

✳For below-sill length (apron-length) curtains, measure to 8 or 10cm below the sill.

✳For floor-length curtains, measure to 1cm above the floor. If there are double curtains, the inner pair should be 1cm shorter than the outer pair.

✳When joining patterned fabric widths, measure the distance between the beginning of one motif and the beginning of the next and add that measurement to the length of each piece of fabric.

HEADINGS AND WIDTH REQUIREMENTS

Each curtain is usually composed of a number of widths sewn together. Choice of heading will affect the amount of fabric you need in order to make the required fullness. This is usually expressed as a multiple of the overall width of the treatment, that is, the length of the track or pole and not the actual width of the window itself.

The simplest headings include the pocket heading, where a rod or tension wire is inserted into a fabric pocket sewn at the top of the curtain, and ties or tab-tops that loop over a pole. Another low-sew option is simply to clip a length of fabric to a rod. These treatments tend to be less full than those described below and are a good way of displaying fabric in flattish panels.

✳Standard gathered headings need one and a half to two times the width of the track.

✳Pencil pleats need two and a half to three times the width of the track.

✳Pinch pleats need two times the width of the track.

✳Box pleats need two and a half to three times the width of the track.

✳Cartridge pleats need two and a half times the width of the track.

TRACKS, RODS AND POLES

Curtains can be hung in a variety of ways. Choosing the means of suspension is another key decision that will affect how a window treatment looks and functions.

✳Track is the utilitarian choice and most types are unobtrusive or designed to be concealed in some way. Tracks can be fixed to the ceiling, to the window frame, or extended beyond the window and attached to the wall. Multi- or double-track systems are available so that you can hang layers of drapery or partner a sheer with a heavier dress curtain. While plastic tracks are standard, metal tracks are also available for hanging heavier fabrics. Angled or shaped tracks allow you to hang curtains at bay and bow windows, while tracks are also available that allow curtains to overlap in the middle.

✳Metal rods are good for hanging sheers and lace panels. Rods that swivel allow you to curtain recessed casements or French windows without interfering with the way the window opens.

✳Wooden and metal rods occupy the decorative end of the spectrum and are very much designed to be seen.

LINING

Lining a curtain improves the way it hangs, increases its insulating properties (sound and heat), blocks light and enhances privacy. Heavier fabrics always benefit from lining, as it helps to hold a curtain's shape. Special blackout lining is available that blocks light completely. You can also use lining in a more decorative sense by partnering two different patterns – one for the dress curtain and a contrasting one for the lining. If you are using plain lining, calculate the amount you need in the same way as for the main fabric, excluding any extra material that you might need to match patterns.

148

floors

Laying a new floor tends to be a job for the professionals, for several reasons. Firstly, considerable physical strength is required to manipulate unwieldy and often heavy materials. Specialist tools are generally needed – and the skills that come only with experience. Flooring materials are often expensive, too, and you will not want to damage them through clumsy handling, or lay the floor so badly that it is an eyesore. If you are reasonably confident of your DIY skills, however, there are a number of jobs you might consider tackling, ranging from sanding and finishing floorboards to laying soft tiles.

Measuring and calculating quantities

As with any decorating job, accurate measurement is essential. Before you start, establish the system of measurement in which your choice of flooring is commonly sold and use the same to take measurements of the area in question. Don't take your measurements in metric and then convert them to imperial or vice versa – you're bound to make mistakes.

✳Measure the area using a steel tape and draw a rough sketch, marking on it the position of doors, windows, fireplaces, alcoves and any other irregularities of contour.

✳Working to a scale of 1:20, transfer the sketch to graph paper.

✳To calculate the surface area, multiply the width of the room by the length.

✳If you are ordering carpet or sheet flooring and want a seamless effect, multiply the width and length at their greatest points. If sheet materials or carpet is not available in rolls wide enough to cover the floor without seams, take your plan to the supplier or fitter who should be able to work out where the seams will go.

✳For other types of flooring, multiply the width and length at their greatest points, then add in the area of alcoves, or subtract the area of built-in fittings. Add 5 per cent for wastage.

✳Some types of flooring, such as tiles, are sold in units. To calculate the quantity you need, divide the total floor area by the area of one tile, adding 5 per cent for wastage. Some flooring materials are sold in packs that specify the area of coverage. In this case, simply divide the floor area by the area covered by each pack to determine how many packs you need.

✳To calculate the quantity of flooring required to cover a flight of stairs, first measure the length by running a piece of string from top to bottom, across each tread and down each riser. Measure the width of each tread to establish the widest and multiply the two dimensions together. Add an extra 60cm if you want to turn the carpet at a later date to even out wear.

Laying carpeting

In large open-plan areas carpet joins are unavoidable but there are ways you can lessen their impact. Before you order the carpet, think about the direction in which you want the rolls to run. In practical and economic terms, the fewer the strips the better. However, if you run the carpet at right angles to the main source of natural light, joins will be less visible; if you run it in the direction of traffic routes, it will last longer. Avoid joins in places such as the top of stairs, where they could become a safety hazard.

✳Joins will be more apparent if you are laying plain rather than patterned carpet.

✳A carpet with a small regular pattern will look better running down the length of the room. When ordering patterned carpet, allow for one matching repeat per strip in the calculations.

Preparing, sanding and finishing existing wooden floors

Many older houses have timber floorboards that can be renovated, finished or decorated for a fraction of the cost of new flooring. In many cases, such floorboards will need to be sanded after basic preparation to remove the dirt, old paint, stains and polish, and to even out the surface. Sanding can be back-breaking work; the machines are heavy and require some skill to use. The work is also noisy and generates a great deal of dust. For an average-sized room you will probably need to allow a couple of days to complete the job, so make sure you hire the equipment for a sufficient length of time.

PREPARATION

✳Go over the floor carefully to assess its condition. If nails have worked their way to the top and are protruding, use a nail punch to sink the nail heads below the surface and fill the holes with stopping. Nail down any loose boards.

✳Fill any large gaps between floorboards with wooden fillets coated with adhesive. Fill small gaps with wood filler. Replace any damaged or split boards completely.

✳If the floor is painted, use a chemical stripper to remove as much of the paint as possible to avoid clogging up the sander. Tackle small paint splashes with a scraper or sandpaper. Wash the floor with hot water and detergent but don't soak it.

SANDING

Most jobs require a drum floor sander, an edge sander and possibly a small disc sander for awkward corners. You will also need sheets of sandpaper in coarse, medium and fine grades.

SAFETY For your own protection, it is essential that you wear a mask and goggles, and possibly ear protectors. The hire shop should supply you with operating and safety instructions – read these carefully and seek advice if there is anything you don't understand. When operating the drum sander, try to keep the flex over your shoulder and fit the power plug into a circuit breaker. Dispose of the sawdust safely: it is highly inflammable and can spontaneously combust if left lying around in rubbish bags inside the home. Never burn sawdust.

✳Start by clearing the room. Cover what you can't remove with dustsheets. Seal doorways with plastic sheeting and open the windows. Sanding generates stupendous amounts of fine dust, so it is advisable to cover sensitive electronic equipment elsewhere in the home.

✳If your floorboards are very battered and uneven, begin sanding with coarse-grade sandpaper. Switch on the drum sander before you lower the sanding surface to the floor. Then keep moving – if you linger in one spot for any length of time, the sander will gouge a hole or depression in the wood. Work across the boards diagonally, then repeat, going in the opposite direction. Then change to medium-grade sandpaper and sand parallel to the boards. Finally, smooth the surface with fine-grade sandpaper, sanding parallel to the boards.

✳If your floorboards are in pretty good condition, don't bother sanding with coarse sandpaper. Sand parallel with the grain/boards, first with medium- then with fine-grade paper.

✳Change the sanding sheets as needed and make sure you empty the dustbag frequently.

✳After you have sanded the main floor area, use an edge sander to tackle the edges. Sand first with a medium-grade disc and then a fine-grade disc. If necessary, use a disc sander to work around tight corners or pipework.

✳After sanding, vacuum, sweep or wipe up all the remaining dust. Go over the floor with white spirit and allow it to dry.

FINISHES FOR WOODEN FLOORS

Wooden floors that have been prepared and sanded require further finishing to protect them from wear and staining. Whichever treatment you choose, try it out on an off-cut or on an inconspicuous area first to assess how it will look under existing conditions of natural light. Bear in mind that many decorative floor treatments take time to apply – you may need to layer on several coats of paint, seal or varnish and allow drying time in between. Before you begin, make sure that the floor is free of dust and grease, and apply knotting solution to prevent knots in the wood from bleeding.

✳*Seals, waxes and varnishes* These treatments preserve the appealing grainy texture and tone of the wood. However, polyurethane seals will yellow as they age and may make pine floorboards look a little glaring. Several coats of natural wax well rubbed in create a soft, mellow, glowing surface.

✳*Wood stains* Tinted stains and varnishes are designed to be applied directly to wood; they soak into the grain and preserve the textural patterning. Apply evenly with a brush, working in the direction of the grain. A stained floor will require further sealing, waxing or varnishing.

✳*Liming agents* Wood can be lightened using a number of liming agents – white paint, proprietary liming wax or gesso. Start by opening up the grain of the wood by scrubbing the boards along the grain with a stiff wire brush. Work the liming agent into the grain with a pad of steel wool, then remove the surplus from the surface with a soft cloth. Seal or wax the floor afterwards.

✳*Paint* Choose between hard-wearing yacht paint, floor paint or oil-based eggshell or gloss. The floor must be primed first and then will need several coats of paint for full coverage, followed by several coats of seal or varnish to protect the surface.

Laying soft tiles

Soft tiles are easier to handle than sheet flooring. The same method applies if you are laying vinyl, lino, cork, rubber or carpet tiles, although the adhesive will vary (and some tiles are self-adhesive). The principal challenge is to work out how to lay the tiles so that you don't end up with a narrow border of cut tiles around the perimeter.

✳Refer to your scale plan to establish the centre of the room. Then loose-lay the tiles in one quarter of the room, starting at the centre and working towards the edges.

✳After you have loose-laid one quarter of the room in whole tiles, examine the gap between the last whole tile and the perimeter. If this is less than half a tile wide, adjust the centre point until you establish a position that will mean the gap is at least half a tile wide.

✳To tile around a corner, place a tile on top of the last whole tile. Then place another tile on top, butted up to the wall. Mark the overlap. The marked strip will show you where to cut to fill the gap. Before cutting, repeat the exercise around the corner, so you only have to cut one tile to fill the gaps.

✳To tile around curved obstacles, make a paper template and transfer the contour to the tile, then cut to fit.

Lighting

A key element in any decorative scheme, lighting directs the eye at whatever is worthy of attention and enhances scale and proportion. Purely decorative lights – those fittings or objects that may not provide much in the way of overall illumination, but serve as focal points in their own right – are an important part of the mix, but they aren't enough by themselves to light a home safely, practically or efficiently. 'Statement' or decorative lighting should be considered within the context of an overall lighting scheme.

Professional help

Some decorative projects are fully within the scope of an amateur – from sourcing right through to final finishes. In the case of lighting, however, it often pays to get professional help. Anyone can buy a light fitting in a shop, take it home and plug it in, but for more complex installations or any work that is required to the lighting infrastructure of circuits, plugs, sockets and switches, you will need to call in an electrician who has the relevant qualifications and accreditations. In some parts of the world – Germany, for example – all electrical work must be carried out by a professional, even wiring plugs. Err on the safe side: electricity is a powerful, potentially lethal force and it's not something to experiment with. As is the case with other trades, a word-of-mouth recommendation can be a useful shortcut to finding the right person for the job.

If you are planning a major overhaul, you may also need help at the design stage, especially if you are considering using LEDs, fibre optics or other specialist light sources. Even if what you are planning is less ambitious, it is still well worth visiting a lighting showroom or lighting design consultancy to gain an appreciation of the effects created by different types of fitting. Some showrooms have room sets with full blackout facilities to enable you to see how various schemes work in practice; many provide design assistance. Never buy a light fitting before you have seen it illuminated – you're buying light, not just a light, and you need to see what it can do: whether the light is diffused, concentrated or directional, for example.

It is also a good idea to research the market to find out about technological developments. Lighting is changing rapidly and you could well find that what you might have ruled out on grounds of expense or disruption has become easier to install and more affordable.

How many lights do you need?

The short answer is probably more than you think. One of the most common mistakes people make in lighting is to rely on too few overbright lights in a given area – in some extreme cases, a single central pendant may be providing most, if not all, of the illumination. This is wrong for two reasons. Firstly, one or two dominant (that is, very bright) fixtures will cause glare, which is tiring for our eyes because they have to work constantly to accommodate the difference between light areas and dark areas. Secondly, relying on a few light sources creates a banal, deadened atmosphere that is not conducive to relaxation.

To give a rough rule of thumb, the average-sized living area needs about four to five separate sources of light to prevent glare and to generate a welcoming, intimate atmosphere.

How much light do you need?

Light is measured in 'lux' ('footcandles' in the United States), which is a calculation of how much light arrives at a given surface. The amount of light that you require in a specific area will depend on what activity you pursue there. You can hire a lux meter if you want to take specific readings of light levels, but the following guidelines will give you a means of comparison:

- 200 lux – living areas.
- 300–500 lux – kitchens and general working areas such as utility rooms.
- 500–750 lux – reading, computer and desk work.
- 1,000–1,500 lux – drawing and detailed work.

Types of light source

The light source – what most of us would call the light bulb or tube – is an important consideration when it comes to choosing lighting. The three principal light sources used in the home are tungsten, halogen and fluorescent, although LEDs are increasingly seen in domestic applications (see page 46).

Decoratively speaking, the chief difference between the three most common sources is one of colour. Tungsten lamps – whether they are in the form of bulbs, tubes, candle bulbs or reflectors – emit a warm, yellowish light that is flattering and intimate. Halogen, both mains- and low-voltage versions, produces a crisp, white light that renders colours more faithfully. Fluorescent tubes used to be notorious for their sickly greenish-tinged light but have recently improved in appearance. Coloured fluorescents are also available.

Lighting infrastructure

Installing new lighting may require changes to your lighting infrastructure. While this is always a job for a professional, it is useful to understand how the basic system works.

In Britain electricity is supplied to each individual home via a distribution box. From that point, a number of fused ring circuits route power to wall sockets and back again. There may also be individual spurs that extend from the ring circuits. Many homes also have separate lighting circuits that take a smaller load. These are generally radial and route power to ceiling fittings and fixtures, with the power controlled by a wall switch.

In other parts of the world, radial circuits are the usual arrangement. These extend from the distribution box and terminate at the last socket.

The simplest alterations to lighting infrastructure include installing more wall sockets to allow for greater flexibility and prevent overload, installing fixed or recessed fittings and replacing standard switches with dimmer controls. More involved (and disruptive) alterations include upgrading aged wiring and installing extra circuits. An extra circuit, say in a living area, can offer the opportunity to group lighting controls so that a number of lights (including table lamps) can be switched on and off both individually and at a master switch positioned at the entrance to the room or some other convenient location.

Creating a lighting scheme

If you are undertaking major work on your home – internal alterations, extensive redecoration or the fitting of new kitchens or bathrooms, for example – it is worth considering lighting as early on in the process as possible. Changes to wiring or circuitry disturb plasterwork and other final wall finishes – sometimes flooring, too – and if you leave decisions too late you may be understandably loath to undo what has only just been freshly completed.

MAKE A PLAN
The starting point, whether you intend to commission a professional designer or will simply require the assistance of an electrician for the installation, is to draw up a plan of the area or areas in question. Start by making a sketch, noting all of the permanent features, such as windows, doors, fireplaces, alcoves and radiators, as well as indicating the position of existing power points, switches and fixed or ceiling light fixtures. Mark on the position of built-in features – kitchen cabinets, for example – as well as any large or dominant pieces of furniture that you do not expect to move. Then take accurate measurements and transfer your sketch to graph paper to make a scale plan.

ASSESS YOUR NEEDS
Use the scale plan to assess the existing lighting conditions at different times of the day and night, under both artificial and natural lighting. If you find it difficult to judge by eye, take photographs of the area without using a flash.

* Are there any areas that are conspicuously underlit? Mark these dark areas on your plan.

* Are there any areas that are overbright or any light fixtures that are causing glare?

* Is there sufficient local light to support working areas – for example, kitchen counters or desktops?

* Is it easy to navigate around the area? Can you control lighting from the door as well as individually?

* What are the best features of the area or room? Do existing lighting arrangements enhance them? Are there decorative features you would like to emphasize?

* How much natural light does the area receive? Is there any way that more natural light could be brought into the interior – through simplified window treatments, internal glazing or mirror, for example?

* Which direction does the main source of natural light (largest window or opening) face? North-facing rooms have even, cool-tinged light. South-facing rooms are warmer but see greater contrasts of light levels throughout the day.

* Do existing arrangements give you the flexibility you need? Would dimmer controls help you to vary the mood? Are there enough power points? Floor-level power points, for instance, give you scope for different furniture arrangements.

* Consider any special requirements – for example, bathrooms generally require sealed fittings to prevent water from coming into contact with electricity.

BASIC DESIGN PRINCIPLES
Try out different effects before you commit to a purchase. You can do this very simply using a number of clip-on spots, table lamps or similar, along with foil, pan lids or other shields to diffuse and direct the light. Get a friend or family member to assist. Add light to dark corners, angle light upwards or downwards, and experiment with different wattages. The following guidelines will give you some ideas to consider when planning a new lighting scheme.

* Create glowing backgrounds by targeting light at the planes of walls and ceilings. Bounce light off the ceiling to increase its perceived height; off a wall to increase the sense of breadth.

* Increase the number of light sources in the room to reduce glare. With an increased number of light sources, wattages don't have to be so high to achieve the correct level of light.

* Emphasize fine features or a decorative display with light. Recessed or concealed fittings are a good way of picking out architectural detail.

* Put chandeliers or central lights on dimmers and choose fittings for their decorative appeal.

* Illuminate conversation areas to generate a sense of intimacy.

* Vary the height of lights around the room to draw the eye from place to place.

* Use dimmers to adjust the balance between natural and artificial light at different times of the day, to create a mood of intimacy or to shift the focus of attention in a multipurpose space, for example in a kitchen/diner.

* Filtered light sources (both natural and artificial) set up intriguing patterns of light and shade that animate the interior. Good examples include slatted blinds and pierced shades.

* Graze light across textured surfaces for depth of character.

* Always combine directional light with background light to avoid glare.

Practical matters

Lighting, of course, is not just there for show; it is the means by which we tackle everyday activities safely in hours of darkness or when natural light levels are low. When you are planning a lighting scheme, you should also consider the following practical matters:

HALLS, STAIRS AND LANDINGS
Lights should be diffused and carefully positioned to avoid glare or obscuring shadows that could cause you to misstep. Make sure the stairs are lit so that you can readily distinguish between treads and risers. In narrow halls or entrances, avoid freestanding lights or table lamps with flexes. Position switches by the entrance and at the top and bottom of the stairs so you don't have to navigate your way in darkness.

KITCHENS
Fixed or fitted forms of lighting make sense in kitchens; plan your arrangement around the existing layout. Kitchen work can be hazardous, so make sure the position and spread of light is carefully judged so that you are not working in your own shadow or dazzled by glare. Avoid using table lamps on or anywhere near the work surface. Put the main kitchen lighting on a dimmer switch if you eat in the same area.

EATING AREAS
Light dining tables so that the light source is concealed when you are sitting at the table. The light should be directed at the centre of the table or along its length, so that it bounces upwards and creates a soft glow. If you are using a pendant, don't hang it too low where it will interfere with views across the table. Dimmers allow you to control the mood according to the occasion.

WORKROOMS

When you are lighting working areas, remember that a computer screen is a light source itself. In this case, you will need good background light – uplighting is ideal – combined with more targeted task light directed at the keyboard or work surface. Bear in mind that you will need between three and five times the amount of light you would find comfortable in a living area or bedroom. The extra boost of illumination can be provided by an adjustable task light.

BEDROOMS

Avoid overhead or central fixtures in bedrooms – they can cause glare, especially when you are lying in bed. Make sure you can control lighting from the door and the bedside; dimmer controls are also invaluable. Bedside lights are more practical if they are adjustable – we tend not to remain in the same position for long when we are reading in bed. In children's rooms avoid freestanding floor lights and make sure table lamps are securely anchored. Keep flexes out of reach. Night lights can offer reassurance if children are frightened of the dark, and they are not bright enough to disrupt sleep.

BATHROOMS

Water and electricity are lethal in combination, so safety is a prime consideration when it comes to bathroom lighting. Stringent regulations apply, which vary from country to country. In the UK lights must be controlled by a pull-cord or a switch outside the room. The same does not apply in the US, where switches are grounded. Fittings that are less than 2.5m from tubs, sinks or showers must be completely enclosed with no exposed metal parts or bulbs. Fully waterproofed fittings are available for showers and wet rooms. Light bathroom mirrors from both sides to avoid heavy shadows on the face.

Safety

If you make a mess of a paint job, you may find yourself out of pocket or having to live with an eyesore; if you attempt to tackle even basic electrical work such as wiring a plug without the know-how, your home and even your life could be at risk. An overloaded socket, a wrongly wired plug, a shade made out of an inappropriate material can all be enough to start a serious fire. Always err on the side of caution and call in an accredited electrician to install lights and carry out electrical work.

❋ Aged wiring is a serious hazard. Among the most common signs that your system may be past its best are fuses that blow frequently and for no discernible reason. If you have cause to suspect that your lighting infrastructure is out of date, call in an electrician to test it for you. After 15 to 20 years, most wiring requires replacement.

❋ Smoke alarms save lives. Fit alarms and check the batteries regularly.

❋ Don't overload sockets or power points or you may cause a fire. Sockets in kitchens and living rooms – where appliances and other equipment are often used – tend to be in high demand. Call in an electrician to fit more sockets rather than rely on extension cables or three-way adaptors; alternatively, have a new circuit installed. This will also avoid the hazard posed by trailing wires and flexes.

❋ Check your lights frequently for any sign of damage or wear. Fraying or worn flexes should be replaced. The same goes for brittle, broken or twisted bulb holders. Electric shock or fire can be caused if the bulb and power source are not in proper contact with one another. Keep bulbs and fittings clean and free of dust and grease.

❋ Always wire plugs correctly and fit them with the recommended fuse. A fuse is designed to blow and cut the power supply to prevent fire: if you fit a plug with a higher-rated fuse, you reduce its effectiveness as a safety measure. Make sure wires are not loose.

❋ Always use a bulb or lamp of the recommended wattage for the particular fitting in question. All new light fittings are labelled to show the maximum wattage that should be used. If you exceed that wattage, you run the risk of burning the fitting, or of causing a fire. Switch off the light before you change the bulb. Let the bulb cool down before you touch it so you don't scorch your fingers, and never change a bulb or reposition a light with wet hands. Avoid touching halogen lamps with bare hands, because grease from fingers can cause damage to the quartz envelope. Replacing a bulb in an awkward or high location is a two-person job. Use a proper ladder and have someone secure it for you.

❋ Some types of light fitting, particularly low-voltage halogen, require transformers to step the power down. These must be installed in dry, well-ventilated areas. Never overload a transformer by exceeding its rating. A 100-watt transformer, for example, will be able to support four 25-watt lamps and no more.

❋ Dimmer controls are also individually rated. Check that the wattage of the dimmer can support the number of lights that it controls.

❋ Always have recessed or fixed lights installed by a professional. You may also need advice as to whether such fittings are practical and safe. Downlights and other recessed fittings need a ceiling void that is big enough to allow ventilation and prevent overheating. In older properties the ceiling void may be dusty, which could pose a fire risk.

❋ Many types of bulbs, but especially tungsten and halogen, generate a considerable amount of heat, which means you need to keep them well away from flammable materials. Cooler light sources include fairy lights and fluorescents, which can be used safely in closer proximity to materials such as paper and fabric.

❋ Exercise caution when you acquire a vintage light from a second-hand source, market or junk shop. Before you go ahead and plug it in, take it to an electrical shop or have it checked over by an electrician to make sure it is safe. You may have to have it rewired or have the bulb holder changed.

Saving energy

Of the total domestic energy consumption, lighting accounts for between 10 and 15 per cent. That amount can be reduced relatively painlessly by up to 80 per cent, which is good for your pocket and good for the environment, too.

❋ Switch it off! Don't leave lights burning in unoccupied rooms.

❋ Clean bulbs, shades and fittings are more energy-efficient.

❋ Make the most of natural light by keeping window treatments simple: opt for blinds or curtains that pull well clear of the glass to allow maximum daylight through.

❋ Lower wattages save energy, but make sure you don't lower light levels below what is safe or practical.

❋ Dimmer controls reduce the power required for tungsten and halogen light sources. Fluorescent lamps, however, are not dimmable.

❋ Perhaps the greatest difference you can make is to substitute compact fluorescent lamps (CFLs) for standard tungsten or halogen bulbs. CFLs last ten times longer and consume 75 per cent less electricity than filament bulbs, which convert most of the energy they consume to heat. The standard domestic light bulb, for example, converts only 5 per cent of the electricity it uses into light – the rest is emitted as heat. CFLs now come in a wide range of shapes and sizes and with bayonet or screw caps, so they can be used in many different types of light fitting. However, they are not dimmable and the quality of light they emit is less attractive.

stockists and suppliers

Wallpaper pattern book

REVIVAL (pp60–1)

Top row left to right:
'Japanese Bamboo', Florence Broadhurst collection, Borderline Fabrics
'London Toile' by Timorous Beasties
'Rajapur' by Cole & Son
'Egrets', Florence Broadhurst collection, Borderline Fabrics

Bottom row left to right:
'Japanese Floral', Florence Broadhurst collection, Borderline Fabrics
'McGegan Rose' by Timorous Beasties
'Williamson', designed by Matthew Williamson, Habitat
'Flamingos' by Cole & Son

MODERN FLORAL (pp62–3)

Left to right:
Kenzan collection, Romo
'Miranda', designed by Rachel Kelly, Interactive Wallpaper
Kenzan collection, Romo
'Flowering Rose', designed by Wayne Hemingway, Graham & Green
'Utopia' from the Decadence collection, Harlequin
'Wilde Crysanthemum' by Osborne and Little

MONOCHROME (pp64–5)

Top row left to right:
'Black Kite' wallpaper-poster by By Hanna
'Cloisonne' by Designers Guild
'Bullet' by Timorous Beasties
'Hulanicki', designed by Barbara Hulanicki, Habitat

Bottom row left to right:
'Vortex' by Interiors Europe
'Flower Power' by Graham & Brown
'Woods' by Cole & Son
'Swallows', designed by Absolutezerodegrees and produced by Flo, Places & Spaces

GRAPHIC (pp66–7)

Left to right:
'Cow Parsley' by Cole & Son
'Woodstock' by Cole & Son
'Passion' from the Decadence collection, Harlequin
'Linear' by Timorous Beasties
'Kiely', designed by Orla Kiely, Habitat
'Mouret', designed by Roland Mouret, Habitat

Fabric pattern book

REVIVAL (pp86–7)

Top row left to right:
Vintage
'Damask 04' by Timorous Beasties
Vintage
'Glasgow Toile' by Timorous Beasties

Bottom row left to right:
Vintage
'Mantua' by Designers Guild
'Vegetable Tree', designed by Josef Frank, Svenskt Tenn
Vintage

GRAPHIC (pp88–9)

Left to right:
Vintage
'Appelsiini', designed by Maija Isola and Kristina Isola, Marimekko
Vintage
'Elokuu', designed by Erja Hirvi, Marimekko
'Tsunami', designed by Anna Danielson, Marimekko
Vintage

MONOCHROME (pp90–1)

Top row left to right:
'Durbar Hall' by Designers Guild
'Tuuli' designed by Maija Isola and Kristina Isola, Marimekko
'Peacock Feathers', black and charcoal on Beech Union, Florence Broadhurst collection, available from Signature Prints, Australia
'Ikeda', Tundra Pond on Hopsack, Florence Broadhurst collection, available from Signature Prints

Bottom row left to right:
'Floral 100', Black on Ottoman, Florence Broadhurst collection, available from Signature Prints
'Kivet' designed by Maija Isola and Kristina Isola, Marimekko
'Bottna', designed by Anna Danielson, Marimekko
'Samovaari', designed by Maija Isola and Kristina Isola, Marimekko

TEXTURED (pp92–3)

Left to right:
'Hoop' wall panel by Anne Kyyro Quinn
'Black lace panel' by Lauren Moriarty
'Leaf' wall panel by Anne Kyyro Quinn
'Cityscape Paris' rug by Hive
Pink vinyl lace tablecloth by Lovely Lovely
'Bold Circles' cushion by Anne Kyyro Quinn

Advice

AMERICAN INSTITUTE OF ARCHITECTS (AIA)
1735 New York Ave, NW, Washington, DC 20006, USA
T: 1-800-AIA-3837
www.aia.org
Directory of architects in the US

AMERICAN SOCIETY OF INTERIOR DESIGNERS (ASID)
608 Massachusetts Ave, NE, Washington, DC 20002-6006, USA
T: +1 (202) 546-3480
www.asid.org
Database for finding an ASID interior designer

ASSOCIATION OF MASTER UPHOLSTERERS AND SOFT FURNISHERS
T: +44 (0)1633 215454
www.upholsterers.co.uk
Contact for details of an upholsterer in the UK

BRITISH INTERIOR DESIGN ASSOCIATION
3/18 Chelsea Harbour Design Centre, Chelsea Harbour, London SW10 0XE, UK
T: +44 (0)20 7349 0800
www.bida.org
On-line database of interior designers and suppliers

CDECOR.COM
www.cdecor.com
Directories of interior designers, sources and showrooms

THE CONSUMERS ASSOCIATION
2 Marylebone Road, London NWI 4DF, UK
T: +44 (0)20 7770 7000
www.which.net
Organization dedicated to helping consumers make the right choice when buying products and services

DESIGN COUNCIL
34 Bow Street, London WC2E 7DL, UK
Tel: +44 (0)20 7420 5200
www.designcouncil.org.uk
The UK's national strategic body for design offers information and advice

ROYAL INSTITUTE OF BRITISH ARCHITECTS
66 Portland Place, London W1B 1AD, UK
T: +44 (0)20 7580 5533
www.riba.org
Directory of registered practices in the UK

Paint

AZKO NOBEL
www.deco.azkonobel.com
www.crownpaint.co.uk
Exterior and interior paints

DULUX
T: +44 (0)870 444 1111
www.dulux.co.uk
Extensive range of exterior and interior paints

FARROW & BALL
249 Fulham Road, London SW3 6HY, UK
T: +44 (0)20 7351 0273
www.farrow-ball.com
Manufacturer of traditional paints and papers

JOHN OLIVER
33 Pembridge Road, London W11 3HG, UK
T: +44 (0)20 7221 6466
www.johnoliver.co.uk
Paints, fabrics and wallpaper; colour-matching service

LEYLAND PAINTS
T: +44 (0)1924 354500
www.leyland-paints.co.uk
Can supply a paint matched to any colour swatch

PAPERS AND PAINTS
4 Park Walk, London SW10 0AD, UK
T: +44 (0)20 7352 8626
www.colourman.com
Colour-matching service; experts in the use of colour in historic buildings

See also Cole & Son, Designers Guild, Paint and Paper Library, and Sanderson

Wallpaper and wall coverings

COLE & SON
Ground Floor 10, Chelsea Harbour
Design Centre, Lots Road, London
SW10 0XE, UK
T: +44 (0)207 376 4628
www.cole-and-son.com
Manufacturers of fine printed wallpaper
with extensive historic archive; new
contemporary and revival ranges;
paint collection

COLEFAX AND FOWLER
110 Fulham Road, London
SW3 6HU, UK
T: +44 (0)20 7244 7427
www.colefax.com
Fabric and wallpaper

DEBORAH BOWNESS
www.deborahbowness.com
Bold hand-printed wallpaper designs
featuring photographic images

GRAHAM & BROWN
T: +44 (0)800 328 8452
www.grahambrown.com
'Flower Power', retro, monochrome,
floral; Hemingway range of wallpapers

HANNA
www.byhanna.com
Swedish collection of contemporary
wallpaper

HARLEQUIN
T: +44 (0)8708 300050
www.harlequin.uk.com
Stylish affordable contemporary
papers, printed fabrics and weaves

HARVEY MARIA
Trident Business Centre,
89 Bickersteth Road, London
SW17 9SH, UK
T: +44 (0)20 8516 7788
www.harveymaria.co.uk
Laminated photographic tiles in natural
patterns; can be used on floors or walls

INTERIORS EUROPE
www.interiors-europe.co.uk
Contemporary wallpaper

MAGSCAPES
T: +44 (0)800 091 7029
www.magscapes.com
Magnetic Receptive wallpaper from
Pepper-mint

MALABAR
T: +44 (0)20 7351 5893
www.malabar.co.uk
Wallcoverings in sisal, jute, bulrush
and rattan

MURASPEC
T: +44 (0)870 511 7118
www.muraspec.co.uk
Paper-backed hessian in 15 colours

NEISHA CROSLAND
8 Elystan Street, London
SW3 3NS, UK
T: +44 (0)20 7584 7988
www.neishacrosland.com
Wallcoverings and textiles in bold
contemporary patterns

PAINT & PAPER LIBRARY
5 Elystan Street, London
SW3 3NT, UK
T: +44 (0)20 7823 7755
www.paintlibrary.co.uk
Contemporary wallpapers by designers
such as Allegra Hicks

RACHEL KELLY
www.interactivewallpaper.co.uk
Designer of 'Long Flowers' and 'New
Shoes' interactive wallpapers with
laser-cut stickers

SANDERSON
Unit G9, Chelsea Harbour Design
Centre, Lots Road, London
SW10 0XE, UK
T: +44 (0)8708 300066
www.sanderson-online.co.uk
Papers and fabrics; holds the William
Morris archive

STAMFORD MURALS
T: +44 (0)7802 497 659
www.stamfordmurals.com
Wallpaper murals and photo murals

WALLPAPERDIRECT
www.wallpaperdirect.co.uk
Leading supplier of wallpapers;
selection includes paper murals with
large-scale imagery

WALLPAPER FROM THE 70S
www.wallpaperfromthe70s.com
German on-line shop supplying original
retro papers

Fabric, textiles and window treatments

AIVEEN DALY
2 Letchford Gardens, London
NW10 68A, UK
T: +44 (0)7801 881925
www.aiveendaly.com
Boutique upholstery with a twist using
vintage fabric or unusual materials

ANNE KYYRO QUINN
Showroom 2.06, OXO Tower Wharf,
Bargehouse Street, London
SE1 9PH, UK
T: +44 (0)20 7021 0702
Textured wall panels, cushions and
other textiles

BENNISON
16 Holbein Place, London,
SW1W 8NL, UK
T: +44 (0)20 730 8076
www.bennisonfabrics.com
English company specializing in hand-
printed fabrics based on the designs of
the original eighteenth- and nineteenth-
century English and French textiles;
suppliers in the UK and US

BORDERLINE
Unit 12, 3rd Floor, Chelsea Harbour
Design Centre, London SW10 0XE, UK
T: +44 (0)20 7823 3567
www.borderlinefabrics.com
Florence Broadhurst collection

THE CLOTH DESIGN STUDIO
T: +44 (0)870 777 5100
www.clothuk.com
Digitally transferred imagery onto
furniture

DESIGNERS GUILD
275/277 King's Road, London
SW3 5EN, UK
T: +44 (0)20 7351 5775
+44 (0)20 7893 7400 for stockists
www.designersguild.com
Strongly directional vibrant fabrics;
flocked wallpapers; paint collection

ECLECTICS
www.eclectics.co.uk
T: +44 (0)845 241 1715
Contemporary made-to-measure
blinds, including Kyoto sliding panels
in 'Rainforest' design. Phone for a
brochure or order on-line

EMMA JEFFS
Surface Material Design, 17 Skiffington
Close, London SW2 3UL, UK
T: +44 (0)20 8671 3383
www.surfacematerialdesign.co.uk
Adhesive window films

LAUREN MORIARTY
Textiles, lighting and interior products
12 Pear Tree Lane, London
E1W 3SR UK
T: +44 (0)20 7481 9939
www.laurenmoriarty.co.uk

LOVELY LOVELY
www.lovelylovely.net
Vinyl lace tablecloths and doilies

MARIMEKKO
16–17 St Christopher's Place, London
W1U 1NZ, UK
T: +44 (0)20 7486 6454
+44 (0)1386 423760 for stockists
www.marimekko.co.uk
Finish textile company founded in
1951; designs now stocked by 800
retailers around the world

MISSONI HOME
Interdesign UK, G30 Chelsea Design
Centre, London SW10 0XE, UK
T: +44 (0)20 7376 5272
www.missonihome.it
Brightly coloured homeware

MULBERRY HOME
322 King's Road, London
SW3 5UH, UK
T: +44 (0)20 7823 3455
+44 (0)20 7623 3455 for stockists
www.mulberry.com
Richly textured fabrics – chenilles and
velvets – as well as plaids, tartans
and checks

OSBORNE AND LITTLE
304 King's Road, London
SW3 5UH, UK
T: +44 (0)20 7352 1456
www.osborneandlittle.com
Producers of bold ornamental fabrics
and papers since 1968

RAPTURE AND WRIGHT
T: +44 (0)20 7498 8073
www.raptureandwright.co.uk
Contemporary fabrics and textiles
including the 'Waimea' range

ROMO FABRICS
Lowmoor Road, Kirkby in Ashfield,
Nottinghamshire NG17 7DE, UK
T: +44 (0)1623 756699
www.romofabrics.com
Modern floral fabrics in silk, satin,
linen and cotton

SIGNATURE PRINTS

www.signatureprints.com.au
Manufacturers of up-market textiles
and wallpapers, including designs
by Florence Broadhurst

SQUINT

65 Redchurch Street, London
E2 7DJ, UK
www.squintlimited.com
Funky upholstered furniture; stocked
by Liberty

THE TEXTILE SOCIETY

www.textilesociety.org.uk
Contact for details of antique textile
markets

TIMOROUS BEASTIES

384 Great Western Road, Glasgow
G4 9HT, UK
T:+44 (0)141 337 2622
www.timorousbeasties.co.uk
Designers of 'Glasgow Toile' and
'London Toile'; wallpapers and fabrics
with a subversive modern edge

THE WHITE COMPANY

8 Symons Street, London
SW3 2TJ, UK
T: +44 (0)20 7823 5322
Mail order: +44 (0)870 900 9555
www.thewhitecompany.com
Household linens

ZOFFANY

T: +44 (0)8708 300350
www.zoffany.com
Famous fabric brand; also produces
wallpapers. Modern interpretations
of period designs

Rugs and carpet

AMAZED

T: +44 (0)1937 832813
www.amazed-rugs.co.uk
Rugs and carpets in natural materials
such as wool, jute, hemp and flax,
following the Japanese tradition of
creating harmony between exterior
nature and interior architecture

ANNETTE NIX

T: +44 (0)7956 451719
www.annettenix.com
Specially commissioned rug designs

CHRISTOPHER FARR

Ground Floor, 6 Burnsall Street,
London SW3 3ST, UK
T: +44 (0)20 7349 0888
www.cfarr.co.uk
Wide range of contemporary rug
designs, including an Artist Collection

CRAIGIE STOCKWELL

T: +44 (0)20 7224 8380
www.craigiestockwellcarpets.com
Handmade rugs and carpets

DEIRDRE DYSON

554 King's Road, London
SW6 2DZ, UK
T: +44 (0)20 7384 4464
www.deirdredyson.com
Top of the range bespoke rugs
designed to match your decor

FEARS AND KAHN

T: +44 (0)1623 882170
www.fearsandkahn.co.uk
Vintage rugs

G H FRITH

Kaydon House, Kinmel Park,
Bodelwyddan, Denbighshire,
North Wales LL18 5TY, UK
T: +44 (0)845 490 0600
www.ghfrith.com
Large selection of handmade rugs

HIVE

Unit 1.02, Oxo Tower Wharf, Barge
House Street, London SE1 9PH, UK
T: +44 (0)20 7261 9791
www.hivespace.com
Interior products, including textured
rugs

LOOPHOUSE

88 Southwark Bridge Road, London
SE1 0EX, UK
T: +44 (0)20 7207 7619
www.loophouse.com
Custom handmade 100 per cent wool
rugs and related products including
wallpaper and accessories

ROGER OATES

I Munro Terrace, Riley Street, London
SW10 0DL, UK
T: +44 (0)20 7351 2288
+44 (0)845 612 0072 for stockists
www.rogeroates.com
Flatweaves, runners and Wilton carpet

THE RUG COMPANY

124 Holland Park Avenue, London
W11 4UE, UK
T: +44 (0)20 7229 5148
www.therugcompany.info
Designer rugs by Paul Smith, Matthew
Williamson, Lulu Guinness and Diane
von Furstenberg, among others

Objects of desire

CATH KIDSTON

51 Marylebone High Street, London
W1U 5AW, UK
T: +44 (0)20 7935 6555
Mail order: +44 (0)870 850 1084
www.cathkidston.co.uk
Pretty retro linen and accessories.
Also kitchen containers and stationery.
500 stockists worldwide, 7 UK stores,
2 US stores

DUTCH BY DESIGN

T: +44 (0)8707 444678
www.dutchbydesign.co.uk
Innovative lighting, clocks, decorative
objects

STUDIO TORD BOONTJE

Studio Tord Boontje S.A.R.L., La Cour,
Route de Graix, 42220 Bourg-Argental,
France
T: +33 (0)4 7739 6604
www.tordboontje.com
Lighting, laser-cut paper curtains and
other designs

THORSTEN VAN ELTEN

22 Warren Street, London
W1T 5LU, UK
T: +44 (0)20 7388 8008
www.thorstenvanelten.com
Furniture, lighting and home
accessories

URBAN OUTFITTERS

200 Oxford Street, London,
W1D 1NU, UK
T: +44 (0)20 7907 0800
www.urbanoutfitters.com
Fashion-led 'apartment' wares.
Stores across the UK and US

Lighting

2PM

T: +44 (0)20 8965 9510
www.2pm.co.uk
Innovative lighting designs

ARCHITECTURAL TILES

T: +44 (0)121 706 6456
www.actiles.co.uk
Terra range of floor tiles inset
with LEDs

ARC LIGHTING

T: +44 (0)1983 523399
www.arclighting.com
Illuminated wall tiles

CAMERON PETERS

The Old Dairy, Home Farm, Ardington,
Wantage OX12 8PD, UK
T: +44 (0)1235 835000
www.cameronpeters.co.uk
The widest selection of fine lighting in
the UK, traditional and contemporary

ELECTRICS LIGHTING AND DESIGN

530 West Francisco Blvd, San Rafael,
CA 94901, USA
T: +1 415-258-9996
www.electrics.com
Modern Italian lighting

GREENE'S LIGHTING

1059 Third Avenue, New York,
NY 10021, USA
T: +1 212-753-2507
Bespoke chandeliers

INNERMOST

T: +44 (0)20 8451 3320
www.innermost.co.uk
Contemporary lighting

JOHN CULLEN LIGHTING

585 King's Road, London
SW6 2EH, UK
T: +44 (0)20 7371 5400
www.johncullenlighting.co.uk
Modern light fittings and individual
design service

KICHLER LIGHTING GROUP

7711 East Pleasant Valley Road,
PO Box 318010, Cleveland,
OH 44131, USA
www.kichler.com
Comprehensive range of lighting

THE LIGHTING CENTER LTD

240 East 59th Street, New York,
NY 10022, USA
T: +1 212-888-8380
www.lightingcenter-ny.com
Lamps, recessed and track fittings

LIGHTFORMS

168 Eighth Avenue, New York,
NY 10011, USA
T: +1 212-255-4464
www.lightformsny.com
Contemporary lamps and lampshades

LIGHTOLIER

631 Airport Road, Fall River,
MA 02720, USA
T: +1 508-679-8131
www.lightolier.com
Contemporary lighting range

LONDON LIGHTING COMPANY

135 Fulham Road, London
SW3 6RT, UK
T: +44 (0)20 7589 3612
www.londonlighting.co.uk
Modern light fittings

MARSTON AND LANGINGER

192 Ebury Street, London
SW1W 8UP, UK
T: +44 (0)20 7881 5717
www.marston-and-langinger.com
Chandeliers

MATHMOS

T: +44 (0)20 7549 2700
www.mathmos.com
Lava lamps and other decorative
fittings; Space Projector projects
coloured shapes on walls, including
'Red Rose' pattern by Timorous
Beasties

MCCOLLIN BRYAN

39 Urlwin Street, London SE5 0NF, UK
T/F: +44 (0)20 7703 2262
www.mccollinbryan.com
Lighting, furniture and objects made to
order, including light Lace Cubes

MOOOI

T: +31 (0)76 578 4444
www.moooi.com
Dutch design company specializing
in lighting and furniture

M S K ILLUMINATION, INC

235 East 57th Street, New York,
NY 10022, USA
T: +1 212-888-6474
www.mskillumination.com
Comprehensive range of fittings

SKK

34 Lexington Street, London
W1R 3HR, UK
T: +44 (0)20 7434 4095
www.skk.net
Innovative lighting designs and
lighting consultancy; LEDs

SWAROVSKI

www.swarovski.com
Austrian crystal company,
manufacturer of chandeliers

One-stop shops and general furnishing stores

ABC CARPET & HOME

888 Broadway, New York,
NY 10003, USA
T: +1 212-473-3000
www.abchome.com
Vintage and contemporary furniture,
upholstery, lighting and accessories.
Branches throughout the US

THE CONRAN SHOP

Michelin House, 81 Fulham Road,
London SW3 6RD, UK
T: +44 (0)20 7589 7401
www.conran.com
Contemporary and classic furniture
and home accessories

In the US:
The Terence Conran Shop,
Bridgemarket, 407 East 59th Street,
New York, NY 10022, USA
T: +1 212-755-9079

CRATE & BARREL

Toll-free: 800-967-6696 for a local store
www.crateandbarrel.com
On-line shopping with a huge selection
of furniture; stores all around the US

HABITAT

196 Tottenham Court Road, London
W1T 7LG, UK
T: +44 (0)20 7631 3880
+44 (0)845 601 0740 for branches
www.habitat.net
VIP range of wallpapers by Barbara
Hulanicki and Matthew Williamson,
among others; reissued design
classics; contemporary lighting

HEAL'S

The Heal's Building, 196 Tottenham
Court Road, London W1T 7LQ, UK
T: +44 (0)20 7636 1666 for branches
www.heals.co.uk
Contemporary furniture, lighting and
homeware

IKEA

255 North Circular Road, London
NW13 0QJ, UK
T: +44 (0)845 355 1141 for branches
www.ikea.co.uk
Swedish superstore selling affordable,
stylish furniture and homeware

In the US:
Toll-free: 1-800-434-4532
www.ikea.com

JOHN LEWIS

Oxford Street, London W1A 1EX, UK
T: +44 (0)20 7629 7711
www.johnlewis.com
Department store with wide range of
furniture, furnishings, fabrics and rugs

LIBERTY

210–220 Regent Street, London
W1R 6AH, UK
T: +44 (0)20 7734 1234
www.liberty.co.uk
Extensive furnishings department, rugs,
contemporary and antique furniture

MUJI

www.mujionline.com
www.muji.co.uk
Japanese 'no-brand' goods. 15 stores
throughout the UK; 6 stores in Paris;
other outlets in Norway and Sweden

POTTERY BARN

Toll-free: 1-888-779-5176
for stores across the US
www.potterybarn.com
Contemporary furniture and homeware

Contemporary furniture

ADVANCE FURNITURE

2525 Elmwood Avenue, Buffalo,
NY 14217, USA
Toll-free: 800-477-2285
www.ContemporaryFurniture.com
Contemporary and Scandinavian
furniture for every room in the home

ARAM

110 Drury Lane, London
WC2B 5SG, UK
T: +44 (0)20 7557 7557
www.aram.co.uk
Contemporary furniture from leading
designers

ARIA

295–296 Upper Street, London
N1 2TU, UK
T: +44 (0)20 7704 1999
www.aria-shop.co.uk
Comprehensive range of furniture
by some of the world's foremost
designers including Philippe Starck,
Ron Arad and Verner Panton

B&B ITALIA

250 Brompton Road, London
SW3 2AS, UK
T: +44 (0)20 7591 8111
www.bebitalia.it
Wide range of furniture from
leading Italian designers

KNOLL

1235 Water Street, East Greenville,
PA 18041, USA
T: 800-343-5665
www.knoll.com
Leading furniture manufacturer
since 1938

PLACES AND SPACES

30 Old Town, London SW4 0LB, UK
www.placesandspaces.com
Contemporary furniture, lighting and
wallpaper collection

PURVES & PURVES

220–224 Tottenham Court Road,
London W1T 7QE, UK
T: +44 (0)20 7580 8223
www.purves.co.uk
Contemporary furniture, lighting and
home accessories

SCP

135–139 Curtain Road, London
EC2A 3BX, UK
T: +44 (0)20 7739 1869
www.scp.co.uk
Manufacturer of furniture by some of
the leading names in British design,
including Matthew Hilton, Jasper
Morrison and Terence Woodgate

SKANDIUM

86–87 Marylebone High Street,
London W1U 4QS, UK
T: +44 (0)207 935 2077
www.skandium.com
Specialists in Scandinavian design

SVENSKT TENN

Strandvagen 5, 114 84 Stockholm,
Sweden
T: +46 (0)8670 1600
www.svenskttenn.se
Furniture and textile designs by
Josef Frank

TWENTYTWENTYONE

274 Upper Street, London
N1 2UA, UK
T: +44 (0)20 7837 1900
www.twentytwentyone.com
Vintage twentieth-century design
furniture and objects, modern reissues
of classics and contemporary furniture
and lighting

VIADUCT

1–10 Summers Street, London
EC1R 5BD, UK
T: +44 (0)20 7278 8456
www.viaduct.co.uk
Sole UK agent for the leading
European companies Driade, e15,
Maarten Van Severen, MDF Italia,
Montis and xO

Vintage furniture

AFTER NOAH
121 Upper Street, London N1 1QP, UK
T: +44 (0)20 7359 4281
www.afternoah.com
Vintage emporium stocking furniture,
lighting and retro accessories

ALFIE'S ANTIQUES MARKET
13–25 Church Street, London
NW8 8DT, UK
T: +44 (0)20 723 6066
www.alfiesantiques.com
Twentieth-century furniture on the
ground floor

BONHAMS
13 Montpelier Street, London
SW7 1HH, UK
T: +44 (0)20 7393 3900
www.bonhams.com
Regular auctions of twentieth-century
classics

DE PARMA & DOMUS GALLERY
15 Needham Road, London
W11 2RP, UK
T: +44 (0)20 7736 3384
www.deparma.com
Italian classics by Gio Ponti and
Fornasetti

EATMYHANDBAGBITCH
37 Drury Lane, London
WC2B 5RR, UK
T: +44 (0)20 7836 0830
www.eatmyhandbagbitch.co.uk
Post-war Scandinavian, Italian and
British furniture

THE MODERN WAREHOUSE
243b Victoria Park Road, London
E9 7HD, UK
T: +44 (0)20 8986 0740
www.themodernwarehouse.com
Twentieth-century furniture on-line.
Showroom open by appointment;
preview evenings once a month

ORIGIN
25 Camden Passage, London
N1 8EA, UK
T: +44 (0)20 7704 1326
Modernist ply furniture from Germany,
Scandinavia and the US

PLANET BAZAAR
397 St John Street, London
EC1V 4LD, UK
T: +44 (0)20 7278 7793
www.planetbazaar.co.uk
An eclectic mix of vintage art, furniture,
lighting and lifestyle accessories
including a wide range of twentieth-
century design classics

Kitchen fittings and fixtures

BULTHAUP
37 Wigmore Street, London
W1 1PP, UK
T: +44 (0)20 7495 3663
www.bulthaup.com
High-quality contemporary fitted and
unfitted kitchens

INTERLUEBKE
www.interluebke.com
German kitchen manufacturer. Check
the website for products as well as
dealers worldwide

MIRARI
www.mirarikitchens.com
International contemporary kitchen
design

PARAPAN
T: +44 (0)113 201 2240
www.parapan.co.uk
Through-coloured fascia material

POGGENPOHL
T: +44 (0)1604 763 482 for
suppliers nationwide
www.poggenpohl.co.uk
Contemporary kitchens

SCIN
130 Bermondsey Street, London
SE1 3TX, UK
T: +44 (0)20 7357 7574
www.scin.co.uk
Digitally printed formica, plus many
other contemporary ideas for surfaces
around the home

SIEMATIC
www.siematic.com
Contemporary kitchen designs
available worldwide

ZINC COUNTERS
High Street, Markington, Harrogate,
North Yorkshire HG3 3NR, UK
T: +44 (0)1765 677808
Zinc, pewter and copper cladding for
tables, counters and fascias

Bathroom fittings and fixtures

AGAPE
via Po Barna, 69, 46031 Correggio
Micheli di Bagnola, San Vito, Milan, Italy
T: +39 (0)376 250 311
www.agapedesign.it
Bathroom products and accessories

ALTERNATIVE PLANS
9 Hester Road, London SW11 4AN, UK
T: +44 (0)20 7228 6460
www.alternative-plans.co.uk
Bathroom fixtures and accessories

ARMITAGE SHANKS
Rugeley, Staffordshire, WS15 4BT, UK
T: +44 (0)154 349 0253
www.armitage-shanks.co.uk
Suppliers nationwide

ASTON MATTHEWS
141–147a Essex Road, London
N1 2SN, UK
T: +44 (0)20 7226 7220
www.astonmatthews.co.uk
Contemporary and traditional
bathrooms and accessories

AVANTE BATHROOM PRODUCTS
Thistle House, Thistle Way, Gildersome
Spur, Wakefield Road, Moreley, Leeds
LS27 7JZ, UK
T: +44 (0)113 201 2240
www.avantebathrooms.com
Contempoary bathroom design

BATHAUS
92 Brompton Road, London
SW3 1ER, UK
T: +44 (0)20 7225 7620
www.bathaus.co.uk
Inspirational modern bathrooms

BATHSTORE.COM
T: 07000 228 478 for a catalogue
www.bathstore.com
Units, fixtures and accessories;
87 branches around the UK

BED BATH AND BEYOND
Toll-free: 1-800-462-3966
www.bedbathandbeyond.com
Everything for the bathroom from
fixtures and fittings to accessories.
Stores around the US

BOFFI
via Oberdan, 70-20030 Lentate
sul Seveso, Milan, Italy
T: +39 (0)362 5341
www.boffi.com
Up-market Italian bathrooms

COLOURWASH
Mail order: +44 (0)20 8944 6456
www.colourwash.co.uk
Up-market bathroom specialists in
the London area

C P HART & SONS
Newnham Terrace, Hercules Road,
London SE1 7DR, UK
T: +44 (0)20 7902 5250
www.cphart.co.uk
Cutting-edge bathroom design and
specification; other branches around
the UK

DORNBRACHT
Köbbingser Mühle 6, D-58640
Iserlohn, Germany
T: +49 (0)2371 433 0
www.dornbracht.com
Manufacturers of sanitaryware

DURAVIT
Werderstrasse 36, 78132 Hornberg,
Germany
T: +49 (0)783 370 0
www.duravit.com
Manufacturers of sanitaryware by
designers such as Starck, Foster and
Sieger Design

DURAVIT USA, INC
1750 Breckinridge Parkway, Suite 500,
Duluth, GA 30096, USA
T: +1 770-931-3575
Toll-free: 888-387-2848

IDEAL STANDARD
The Bathroom Works, National
Avenue, Kingston Upon Hull
HU5 4HS, UK
T: +44 (0)1482 346461 for suppliers
www.ideal-standard.co.uk
Innovative contemporary bathrooms

VILLEROY & BOCH
Corporate Headquarters, PO Box
1120, D 66688, Mettlach, Germany
T: +49 (0)686 481 0
www.villeroy-boch.com
Manufacturer of bathroom products

In the UK:
267 Merton Road, London
SW18 5JS, UK
T: +44 (0)20 8871 4028

WATERWORKS
469 Broome Street, New York,
NY 10013, USA
T: +1 212-966-0605
www.waterworks.com
Impeccable style and quality
craftsmanship across a wide range
of prince ranges and designs

Index

acetate 111, 146
acrylic 43, 45
alcoves 31, 48, 72, 75
Anaglypta 75
angora 105
armchairs 96

backlighting 45, 138
baffles 46
bathrooms
    colour in 43, 54
    large patterns 70
    lighting 152
    wallpaper 75
bathtubs 48, 54
bed linen 11, 96, 104, 105, 106
bedrooms
    fabrics 104–7
    lighting 152
    mixing the ingredients 11
    rugs 115
beds 104, 106
bedspreads 96, 105
bedsteads 11
Bell, Vanessa 85
Bey, Jurgen 125
Biba 59
black 24, 26
blinds 35, 108, 110
    roller 138
    Roman 138
Broadhurst, Florence 61
brocade 24, 59, 99, 110, 146

cambric 146
canvas 146
carpets 32, 112, 115
    laying 148
cashmere 105
ceilings, painting 144
chairs 138
    dining 129
    Eames 119
    kitchen 11
    and loose covers 99
    and materials 95, 99, 103
    Panton 119
    plastic (Robin Day) 131
    reupholstery 102
    Victorian 102
chaise longues 138
chandeliers 7, 122
chenille 99
chimney breasts 31
china, patterned 119
chintz 146
cladding 54, 84
cold cathode 46
Cole & Son 11, 59
collectables 126–31
collections 134
colour
    accent versus background 17
    broken 34–9

coloured planes 30–3
complementary colours 19
cool 17, 96
dark 24, 106
neutral 22
practical 52–5
restricted tonal palette 14, 50
return of 14–15
samples 19, 32
see-through 40–5
soft 15
strong 15, 26, 31, 63
swatches 19, 32
warm 17, 96
colour schemes 18–29
    bright palette 22–3
    dark palette 24–5
    metal palette 26–9
    nature palette 20–21
coloured light 46–51
    ambient colour 50
    bathe in colour 48
    coloured fluorescent tubes 46
    colourwashing 48
    LEDs 46
    paths of colour 48
colourwashing 48
colour wheel 19
computer technology 93
concrete 32, 84
cooking ranges 52
coordinated schemes 78
cornice 79
cotton 75, 99, 106, 146
    Egyptian 104, 106
    Madras 36
countertops 35, 36, 84
crochet 93, 95
cupboards, colour 43, 54
curtains 96, 108
    coordination 78
    length 110
    lining 147
    net 110
cushions 22, 99, 105, 106
    covers 96, 101
    floor 138
    making a basic square cushion
        146–7

dado rail 79
damask 59, 75, 99, 146
Day, Robin 131
Delaunay, Sonia 85
design gallery 137–8
desks, metal 129
digital prints 137–8
dimmer controls 50, 151
dishwashers 52
display 134
Dixon, Tom 125
doors 43, 54
dress material 96
Droog Design 125

Dufy, Raoul 85
dupion 146
durries 115

Eames, Charles and Ray 119, 126
eating areas, lighting 151
embroidery 96, 105
energy saving 152
extensions, glazed 43

fabrics see material world;
    soft furnishings
fairy lights 122
fanlights 43
fashion 59, 61
felt 93
fibre optics 122
filing cabinets 28
flock 70, 75
floorboards
    painted 112
    stained 20, 24
flooring
    colour 32
    existing wooden floors 148–9
    hardwood 11
    laying carpeting 148
    laying soft tiles 149
    materials 112–15
    measuring and calculating
        quantities 148
    pale wood 14
    plain 106
    tiles 32, 48
floral patterns
    fabrics 105, 106
    floral branches covered in
        LEDs 122
    wallpaper 62–3
Florence, Linda 75
fluorescent tubes, coloured 46
foils 26, 67, 70, 75
footstools 99, 138
friezes 79
furniture
    metallic schemes 26
    modern 131
    strong colour 22
    upholstered 99, 138
    vintage 126, 129

gels, coloured 45, 46
geometric forms 35, 91, 96, 105, 115
gingham 146
glass 84
    coloured 43
    stained 41, 43
gold-leaf finishes 26, 28
granite 24
Grant, Duncan 85
graphic patterns
    material 88–9
    wallpaper 66–7
grass wall covering 75

green 20
Habitat 131
hallways 31, 70, 115, 151
Hammerite 28
handcrafted work 93
hand-gilding 75
handrails 122
headboards 105, 106, 122
headings (window dressing)
    110, 111, 147
hessian 75
holland 146
Hulanicki, Barbara 59, 61

Isola, Maija 89

Jack light (Tom Dixon) 125
Jacobsen, Arne 126
Jacquard 99
Juicy Couture 59
Jute 75

Kelly, Rachel 75
Kendall, Tracy 70
kilims 115
Kishimoto, Eley 59
kitchens
    colour 54
    counters 35, 36
    doors, drawers and decor
        panels 54
    lighting 151
    mixing the ingredients 11
    units 11
    wallpaper 75
knitted work 84, 93, 95, 96

lace 84, 93, 146
Lace Cube (McCollin Bryan) 125
lacquer 24
laminate 36, 54, 137
landings, lighting 151
laser-cutting 93
leather 93, 99
LEDs (light-emitting diodes)
    7, 46, 48, 122
lighting 120–5, 129
    backlighting 45, 138
    coloured light 46–51
    creating a lighting scheme 151
    decorative light 125
    diffused 108, 110
    how many lights do you need?
        150
    how much light do you need? 150
    infrastructure 150–1
    light shades 26, 45
    natural light 96
    points of light 122
    practical matters 151–2
    professional help 150
    projected 125
    safety 152
    saving energy 152

statement lights 118–19
string lights 122, 152
types of light source 150
Light Shade Shade (Jurgen Bey
and Droog Design) 125
light show 125
Lincrusta 75
linen 75, 99, 104, 106, 146
lino 32, 112
'Long Flower' wallpaper panel
(Rachel Kelly) 75
loose covers 99

McCartney, Stella 59
McCollin Bryan 125
mantelpieces 122
Marimekko 89
material pattern book 86–93
graphic 88–9
monochrome 90 1
revival patterns 86–7
textured 92–3
material world 82–115
bedrooms 104–7
choosing bed linen 106
putting the look together 106
what the well-dressed bed is
wearing 105
comfort zone 99–103
loose or close-fitting? 99
material considerations 99
upholstery options 99
using big prints 99
floors 112–15
colour and pattern underfoot
112
floor-level art 115
placement 115
quality 115
mix and match 94–7
matching patterns 96
mixing patterns 96
as soundproofing 84–5
windows 108–11
window dressing 110–11
see also soft furnishings
MDF (medium-density
fibreboard) 54
melamine 36, 54
metallic finishes 26–9, 67
mirror 26, 125
mix and match 11
furniture 129
textiles 89, 94–7
modernism 7, 8, 58
moire silk 146
monochrome patterns
material 90–1
wallpaper 64–5
moquette 99
'Morphic Damask' wallpaper
design (Linda Florence) 75
Morris, William 68
murals 80–1
muslin 146

neon 46

objects of desire 116–39
21st-century collectables
126–31
details 132–9
design gallery 137–8
digital transfer 137
room for display 134
lighting 120–5
open-plan layouts 72, 76, 112
optical inks 70, 75
organdie 146

paint
applying 144
charts 15, 32
choosing 32
colour planes 32
emulsions 32
floor 32, 112
gloss 26, 112
metallic 26, 28
pigment 32
sample pots 32
types of 144
paint rollers 28, 144
panels
backlit 45, 111
coloured 43, 45
digital prints 138
Panton, Verner 119, 126
paper
digital transfer 137
lining 32
Parapan 54
partitions 43, 75
pelmets 110
Perspex 43, 45, 46
picture rails 79
pillowcases 105, 106
pillows 105
planning the work 142
plasterwork 31, 76, 84
plastic 93, 131
poles, curtain 110, 147
polyester 146
polypropylene 131
practicalities 140–52
floors 148–9
lighting 150–2
painting walls and ceilings 144
papering walls 145
planning the work 142
preparing surfaces for
decoration 143
soft furnishings 146–7
psychedelia 67, 70

quilts 105

'Rajapur' paisley print 11
rattan 20, 75
recesses 31, 46, 48
rectilinear motifs 67
refrigerators 52, 54
retro 24, 36, 67, 126
revival patterns
material 86–7

wallpaper 60–1
rods, curtain 110, 147
room dividers 72, 75
rubber 32, 84, 112
rugs 22, 84, 101, 112, 115
runners 115

Saarinen, Eero 126
safety 143, 152
sateen 146
satin 104, 105, 146
scarves, silk 96
screens 35
sewing 95, 99, 105
sheer materials 110, 111
shower cubicles 48
shutters 110
silk 96, 104, 105, 111, 146
moire 146
silver-leaf finishes 26, 28
sinks 48, 54
sisal 75
skirting boards 79
slate 24
Smith, Paul 11, 59
sofas 96, 99, 101, 102, 103
soft furnishings
making a basic square cushion
146–7
types of fabric 146
windows and blinds 147
see also material world
sound insulation 75, 84–5, 115
splashbacks 36
spots 39
stained glass 41, 43
stairs 115, 151
stairwells 122
steel 84
stone 84
storage units 43, 45
stripes 36, 37
suede 99
suiting materials 99
symmetrical designs 96

tablecloths 96
tables, dining 115, 129, 151
tab tops 110
taffeta 146
tea towels 96
textiles see material world
textured finishes 67
textured material patterns 92–3
throws 96, 105
ticking 36, 146
ties 110
tiles 84
cork-backed 75
digital transfer 137
floor 32, 48, 75, 112
laying soft 149
paths of colour 48
Timorous Beasties 87
toile de Jouy 7, 87
tracks, curtain 110, 147
trompe l'oeil 80

tufted materials 93, 96,
115
tweed 99

underlay 115
upholstery 95, 96, 99, 102–3,
138

valances 110
velour 99
velvet 99, 110, 146
vinyl 32, 75, 112
voile 146
viscose 146

wall hangings 138
wallpaper 56–81
art-house 75
cover-ups 76–9
double-width 75
dramatic return of 58
and fashion 59, 61
flock 70, 75
focal points 72–5
foils 26, 67, 70, 75
hand-printed 75
hanging 145
machine-printed 75
murals 80–1
natural fibres 75
print dynamics 68–71
screen-printed 75
stripping 143
toile de Jouy 7
water-resistant 75
wallpaper pattern book 60–7
graphic 66–7
modern floral 62–3
monochrome 64–5
revival 60–1
walls
coloured planes 31–2
cork-backed tiles 75
fabric treatment 75
geometric motifs 35
gold/silver leaf 28
matching patterns 96
matt black 24
metallic schemes 26
neutral 22
painting 144
papering 145
plain 106, 125
preparing 143
types of wall coverings 75
white 14, 75, 125
wardrobes 106
white goods 7, 52
Williamson, Matthew 59, 61
window treatments 45, 96,
110–11, 147
windows 43, 45, 108
measuring 147
wood, polished 84
woollen fabrics 99
workrooms, lighting 152
woven fabrics 95, 96

Acknowledgements

The publisher would like to thank the following photographers, agencies and companies for their kind permission to reproduce the photographs in this book: 2–3 from left to right Habitat, Romo, Rachel Kelly/Interactive Wallpaper, Habitat, Anne Kyyro Quinn, Vintage fabric, Marimekko, Vintage fabric; 4 Timorous Beasties; 6 Polly Wreford/Narratives; 8–9 Beth Evans (Interior design: Gerardine & Wayne Hemingway of Hemingway Design); 10 Ray Main/Mainstream Images (Echo Design); 12–13 Beth Evans (Interior design: Gerardine & Wayne Hemingway of Hemingway Design); 16 Luke White/Interior Archive (Architect: Sanei Hopkins); 17 Tom Leighton/Livingetc/IPC Syndication; 18–19 Tim Evan Cook/Red Cover; 21 Winfried Heinze/Red Cover; 23 Wilfried Overwater/Taverne Agency (Stylist: Rosa Lisa); 25 Beth Evans (Owner: Nikki Tibbles of Wild at Heart Interiors); 27 Verity Welstead/Livingetc/IPC Syndication; 28 Jake Curtis/Livingetc/IPC Syndication; 29 Luke White/Interior Archive (Designer: Julian Meath Baker); 30–1 Vincent Leroux/Marie Claire Maison (Stylist: Catherine Ardouin, Architect: Carl Frederic Svensted); 32 left Per Gunnarsson (Interior Designer: Lena Widenfelt); 32 centre Gaelle Le Boulicaut (Designer: Prisque Salvi); 32 right Pia Ulin (Stylist: Cilla Ramnek); 33 Hufton & Crow/View (Architect: ACQ Architects); 34 Catarina Costa Cabral (Stylist: Pedro d'Orey, Interior Design: Mónica Penaguião); 36 courtesy of Scin Ltd; 37 left Gaelle Le Boulicaut (Interior Designer: Nicolas Robert); 37 right Dexter Hodges/Medita (Architect: Julia Schulz-Dornburg); 38 Ray Main/Mainstream Images; 39 Mark Luscombe-Whyte/Interior Archive (Designer: Eric Gizard Ass.); 40 Bill Smith/Livingetc/IPC Syndication; 41 Mark Luscombe-Whyte/Interior Archive (Designer: Pip Isherwood); 42 Vercruysse & Dujardin (Stylist: Kat de Baerdemaeker); 44 Mark Luscombe-Whyte/Interior Archive (Designer: Eric Gizzard Ass.); 45 Graham Atkins Hughes/Red Cover; 46 Jefferson Smith/Arcblue (Architects: Tonkin Liu Ltd); 47 Ray Main/Mainstream Images; 48 Darren Chung/Mainstream Images (Ice Cube Design); 49 Rachael Smith; 50 Mel Yates; 51 Jake Fitzjones (Furniture designer: Lucho Brieva); 52 left Jake Curtis/Livingetc/IPC Syndication; 52 above right Lucinda Symons/Ideal Home/ IPC Syndication; 52 below right Jake Fitzjones (Fourneaux de France); 53 Jan Baldwin/Homes & Gardens/IPC Syndication; 54 Christian Sarramon/Zapa Images; 55 Simon Whitmore/Livingetc/IPC Syndication; 56–7 Edina van der Wyck/Interior Archive (Designer: Marion Cotterill); 69 Gaelle Le Boulicaut (Interior Designer: Jason Mclean, wallpaper designed by Eley Kishimoto); 70 left Reto Guntli/Zapa Images; 70 right Holly Jolliffe; 71 Jefferson Smith (Wallpaper by Timorous Beasties); 73 Catherine Gratwicke/Livingetc/IPC Syndication; 74 Gaelle Le Boulicaut (Architect: Jake Dowse, Interior Designer: Luc Dowse); 76 Ray Main/Mainstream Images (Jocelyn Warner Design); 77 Jason Loucas/GB Productions (Interior Designer: Greg Natale); 78 James Mitchell/Red Cover;

79 Sophie Munro/Red Cover; 80 Tim Evan-Cook/Red Cover (Architect: Sarah Featherstone, Featherstone Associates); 81 Ray Main/Mainstream Images (Designer: Jo Warman); 82–3 Adrian Briscoe/Livingetc/IPC Syndication; 94 Vincent Leroux/Temps Machine/Marie Claire Maison (Stylist: Catherine Ardouin); 95 Alun Callender/Red Cover (Decorated by Petra Boase); 97 Jason Loucas/GB Productions (Interior Designer: Greg Natale); 98 Visi/Camera Press; 100–1 Beth Evans (Owner: Nikki Tibbles of Wild at Heart Interiors); 102 Stephen Perry/Livingetc/IPC Syndication; 103 James Merrell/Homes & Gardens/IPC Syndication; 104 Juan Hitters/Surpressagencia (Stylist: Mariana Rapoport, Architect: Mishal Katz & Sebastián Fernández); 105 above Verity Welstead/ Livingetc/IPC Syndication; 105 below Stephen Perry/Livingetc/IPC Syndication; 106 Jake Fitzjones (Interior Designer: Rachel Harding); 107 Jason Loucas/GB Productions (Interior Designer: Greg Natale); 108 Jefferson Smith (Soft furnishings by Timorous Beasties); 109 Graham Atkins Hughes/Red Cover; 110 left Jake Curtis/Livingetc/IPC Syndication; 110 right courtesy of Eclectics; 111 above Emma Jeffs; 111 below Catherine Gratwicke/Livingetc/IPC Syndication; 112 left Richard Powers (Interior Designer: Greg Natale); 112 right Dan Duchars/Red Cover; 113 Renee Frinking/Sanoma; 114 Ray Main/Mainstream Images (Designer: Missoni); 115 Daniela Mac Adden/Surpressagencia (Stylist: Mariana Rapoport, Architect: Saban-Grin); 116–17 Fabienne Delafraye/Maison Madame Figaro/Camera Press; 120 Francis Amiand/Maison Francaise/Camera Press; 121 left Tim Evan-Cook/Red Cover; 121 right Bridget Peirson/Homes & Gardens/IPC Syndication; 122 Tom Leighton/Livingetc/IPC Syndication; 123 Lisbett Wedendahl/House of Pictures; 124 Fabienne Delafraye/Maison Madame Figaro/Camera Press; 125 above courtesy of McCollin Bryan; 125 below courtesy of Studio Jurgen Bey produced by Moooi; 127 Ray Main/Mainstream Images (Designer: Andrew Weaving); 128 A/Baralhe/Photozest; 129 left Dave Young; 129 right & 130 Holly Jolliffe; 131 Beth Evans (Owner: Nikki Tibbles of Wild at Heart Interiors); 132 Hotze Eisma/Taverne Agency (Stylist: Reineke Groters); 133 left Philippe Kress/House of Pictures; 133 right Sofie Helsted/House of Pictures; 134 above S Clement/Photozest; 134 below Catherine Gratwicke/Livingetc/IPC Syndication; 135 Louis Lemaire/Sanoma; 136 Tom Leighton/Livingetc/IPC Syndication; 137 Xavier Béjot/Tripod Agency; 138 courtesy of Cloth UK; 139 Happyliving.dk/House of Pictures; 140–1 Wilfried Overwater/Taverne Agency (Stylist: Rosa Lisa).

Every effort has been made to trace the copyright holders. We apologize in advance for any unintentional omissions and would be pleased to insert the appropriate acknowledgement in any subsequent edition.